WHAT IS LANDSCAPE?

Traditional if now bewildered landscape: an old dike fronting reclaimed land sliced with gutters, bordered by afforested dunes, and opening on estuarine tides and coastal sky. JRS

WHAT IS LANDSCAPE?

JOHN R. STILGOE

The MIT Press   Cambridge, Massachusetts   London, England

This book was set in Trajan Pro 3 and Adobe Garamond by the MIT Press. Printed and bound in the United States of America.

Library of Congress Cataloging-in-Publication Data is available.
ISBN: 978-0-262-02989-6

10 9 8 7 6 5 4 3 2 1

For
Jack M. Stilgoe

CONTENTS

Hollandsch Molen Landschap.

Quintessential 1900 Frisian/Dutch landscape: a path-topped dike, a tide gate, reclaimed pasture pumped by a windmill, a farmstead, all beneath a tremendous sky. (Author's collection.)

PREFACE

Landscape is a noun. First. It designates the surface of the earth people shaped and shape deliberately for permanent purposes. Oceans, polar ice, glaciers, rocky islets, and—even today—parts of steppes, deserts, tropical forest, and similar places seemingly untouched (or at least uninhabited, perhaps seldom if ever transited) are properly wilderness. A soda can tossed from an airplane mars the polar ice just as it mars the ocean, but the dropped can converts neither spot into landscape. As an adjective, "landscape" names a genre of painting and other representational art more or less centered on views of the solid surface of the earth. Now used loosely to include wilderness other than the deep sea (**seascape** exists for that), among art historians and amateur photographers the word raises the issue of proportion: overwhelming background converts portrait or still life into landscape image. As an adjective, "landscape" also designates types of architecture and building: landscape architecture and landscape gardening find core identities in ground shaped for beauty rather than shelter and crops. As a verb, "landscape" means to install plants (chiefly sod but also bushy coniferous shrubs and scraggly trees) on raw land recently covered thinly with loam and more or less smoothed. This book offers a compact analysis of "landscape" as noun stripped of accessory and ornament, the word naming the skeleton and sinews of shaped land.

This book also offers mostly words, and mostly old ones, at first glance simple but on reflection nuanced and rich. Putting names to core components of landscape troubles at first and then empowers. **Meadow** names made openness, a different kind from **pasture**. One produces hay for winter feed, the other offers summer grazing: both differ from that favorite of landscape painters and landscape architects, the glade. Both figure prominently in preschool picture books depicting farms as nineteenth-century mixed-use, Old MacDonald places, but as background only, landing strips for sunlight. Toddlers learn the sounds made by cows and sheep, not the attributes of meadows and pastures, let alone the names of flat or rolling greensward. Any thoughtful explorer of landscape musing on landscape constituents muses mostly in words, if only to wonder silently at the names of things. A reader discovering in a novel or travelogue the term **oriel window** can look up the words in a good dictionary, especially an illustrated architectural dictionary, and can proceed somewhat reassured. Yet a walker noticing an elaborate sort of bay window that seems to have been built off-site finds researching the construct perplexing. Inquiring into what is noticed visually means getting the details into words, and often getting tired or lost in the process. Finding that lexicographers rarely distinguish between **ditch** and **trench** (and thus ignore nuances implicit in **trench coat**) disappoints at first but then (sometimes) sparks self-driven determination. Most explorers, even the most casual ones improving their time by staying away from stores, coffee shops, and electronic devices, can name the essential components of landscape and begin to wonder at nameable nuance. They can look up terms in good dictionaries, especially old ones.

Dictionaries travel badly. Most are heavy and retard the explorer of landscape. But they reward homecoming. Secondhand unabridged ones are cheap to acquire. Atlases, gazetteers, and specialized maps remain expensive: while they shame electronic cartography, they can bankrupt. They travel badly too, especially in rain. Being lost, even being deliberately free of electronic location devices, sharpens one's senses and often eventually reassures. Making one's way often reveals paths distinct and well used or hard to discern, abandoned (perhaps for good reason), but all nonetheless instructive. Exploring, being lost for a while, looking around without distraction, or just going for a walk eventually raises questions of words, if only in the telling and retelling of short-term adventure. Almost anyone can afford an unabridged dictionary, even an older one (which often proves more insightful), and therefore can explore the origins of basic landscape terms and discover the wealth in root and period meaning implicit in terms so seemingly simple, so easy to spell, so fundamental to learning to speak and read English that they enter the mind as concept foundation stones buried and almost forgotten. Using an older unabridged dictionary often leads to coveting new ones, even the most recent twenty-volume edition of the *Oxford English Dictionary*—one of the chief sources of this little book—open volumes of which can be placed side by side for comparative analysis. But older dictionaries offer possibilities all their own. In them the inquirer finds definitions, even headwords, now gone from all but a few contemporary dictionaries. Serendipitous discovery leads to reading in etymological dictionaries and in dialect and other specialist lexicons, and in listening ever more carefully to people close to landscape constituents, people who distinguish **gut** from **gat** and both from **gutter** and **guzzle**.

British dictionaries typically focus on word history and even today emphasize the needs of well-educated, upper-class, often scholarly readers. The *Chambers Dictionary* still champions Scottish attitudes against the English *Oxford English Dictionary*: neither nods to blue-collar readers. American dictionaries have always emphasized correct current usage: they deemphasize class distinction while facilitating class mobility (hopefully upward) and the assimilation of immigrants learning English. American lexicographers have proven more open to valuing spoken English, but since the 1960s triumph of television, the news announcer and broadcast speech have dismissed many of the regionalisms, Africanisms (including those from the Bahamas), and ruralisms which shaped a century of Webster and Merriam-Webster unabridged dictionaries (all often available for a pittance at flea markets and in used-book shops) and which graced the now-forgotten twelve-volume *Century Dictionary* of 1914. At some point on a sandy beach or among commercial fishermen, or even aground in a small boat, the careful inquirer may hear a word pronounced **swatch** but spelled otherwise in most English and American dictionaries. **Swash** is a hard word and abscondite. But asking a local commercial fisherman about a stretch of low-tide water snaking through sandbars often produces it, and once heard, it opens on mazy usage and lexicography.

Two keys unlock essential landscape. Looking around, walking and noticing and thinking, putting words to things, especially simple things, enables and empowers and pleases: discovering landscape is inexpensive, good exercise for body and mind, and leads to satisfying and often surprising discovery. Swedish has a term for the restorative, relaxing effect of being solitary and thoughtful, but not lonely: **ensamhet**. Asking generally, eschewing what seem generic terms, produces localisms, archaisms, and glimmering portals, especially from people intimate with a local place. "What is that?" asked in a polite, genuine way with a tentative gesture toward some landscape component often produces rich response: "Well, it's not really a slough, not really, it's a bayou, you can get through at the end there, in a canoe, at least some kids did a couple of years ago." In a nation using all too casually old spatial and structural words, the scattering of Dutch, French, and Spanish terms proves elusive until one points at scrub in southwest Colorado, asks, and hears **bosque** in response. Questing without generic landscape terms makes questioning almost magic. But first one must see something, must realize it, must make it real, then ask carefully and listen well, maybe ask again, and later on, feet up, look up words.

So here find a little book (with bibliographical ballast) about some words critical in naming the essence of landscape. Neither dictionary nor field guide, it is only an invitation to walk, to notice, to ask, sometimes to look up and around, sometimes to look up in a dictionary. It belongs at home. Pockets are for energy bars, apples, chocolate, and the smallest of notebooks. But where landscape flourishes in its most essential form, pockets prove few.

Impermanence rules the sandy marge: dunes form, move, sometimes linger, occasionally erode in great gales or hurricanes, make untenable anything but temporary human building, remind the wise of natural-system force. JRS

INTRODUCTION

Landscape smells of the sea. Wading into the ocean on a summer day reveals the essence of landscape. Seaward lie deeper water, surf, riptides and undertow, ocean rollers, and an arc of horizon never still and mocking human control. Landward the beach glows in sunlight, interrupting the storms which sweep sand and dunes and smooth cobbles and boulders. Like the margin between the end of type on this page and the edge of the page itself, every beach is marginal, literally the **marge**, a limicole zone contested by wilderness and human order. With back to the sea, the wader sees sand and seawalls, as well as cottages and hotels and pathways that are beyond the reach of all but hurricanes and incremental sea level rise. Somewhere in that space lies the ragged edge of what most people too casually dismiss as landscape, the controlled spatial and structural construct, permanent (presuming ceaseless maintenance and continuous renewal), the common built form easily taken for granted, all too easily half seen.

Children upend crenellated pails of wet sand and sur-
round their castles with moats and dikes, roads and walls, but
only the youngest presume permanence. Tides come in and
swallow. Sometimes children cut gateways in embankments
and walls, inviting the flood tide: sometimes they shovel furi-
ously against it, throwing up sand in futile fun. Playing with
plastic pails and tiny shovels in sand and salt water and sunlight, they learn what **landscape** designates, experience
directly the making of what essential landscape is.

"Landscape" comes from the old Frisian language of
what is now the coast of the Netherlands and the North Sea
coast of Germany. Skewed and co-opted by individuals and
cohorts with their specialized, narrow interests, the word
once meant **shoveled land**, land thrown up against the sea.
Schop is an old word still vibrant in modern Dutch: it
means shovel.[1] Seamen introduced **landschop** to sixteenth-
century alongshore Englishmen who misunderstood or
mangled its pronunciation but retained its meaning in **landskep**, at least for a while.

Of course pail and shovel teach more. The crenellated
pail makes conical, rampart-topped castles, one of the oldest
icons of order, possession, responsibility, and maintenance,
today often topped by fluttering iridescent pinwheels. Its
bail demonstrates the ancient rule of path and road making.
It is the same length whether lying flat on the pail rim or
held upright; but a way curved around a hill tires people and
draft animals far less than one aligned over the summit. **Rim**
too is an old word, rooted in the Old Norse **rimi** and Old
English **rima** meaning a strip of raised land: such strips not
only drained better in wet areas but acted as **dams** or **dikes**,

keeping water in or out. Bail and rim, both curved, reflect the strength of curves: the Old Norse **beygla**, meaning hoop, produced the English word for horseshoe-shaped things supporting or containing anything (even the necks of oxen) but also a synonym for **pail**.[2] Medieval Englishmen used **bail** and **pail** almost interchangeably, the former term perhaps emphasizing more ordered containment—which is why **bailiffs** kept order in castles and keep courts in order still, and mariners and attorneys bail out seawater and the arrested. But "pail," a word rooted in Old English and Old French confusion about measures and pans, meant a hand tool. **Bucket** connotes a heavier pail used for drawing up water from wells and the sea, usually by winches or windlasses. While English speakers everywhere, and especially Americans, use the two words interchangeably, **pail** or **sand pail** prevails on beaches not so much as local usage but from site-specific tradition. Children too weak to carry buckets make do with pails.

The modern English **shovel** originates from the same roots as **scoop** and **shove** and remains etymologically awkward, but beach toy manufacturers now supply scoops along with shovels and pails, but not yet **skips**, flat, slab-sided scoops familiar to manufacturers of earth-moving equipment.[3] British English designates the result of shoveling, scooping, and shoving as **skips**, what Americans call **piles**. Dumping sand or loam from a pail or truck produces in England a **tip**, from **tip cart**, but in America it creates only a pile. Pails and buckets, as well as skips and piles and tips, figure only slightly in the speech and writing of educated people, while lexicographers typically ignore the nuances of such terms in the spoken language of the poor and illiterate. Especially they ignore the terminology and pronunciation of poor people only loosely tied to locale, especially seafarers.[4]

What sixteenth-century mariners pronounced as "landschop" to uneducated alongshore Englishmen became in time **landskap** or **landskep**, then **landskip**, then **landscape**. If lexicographers focus on the pronunciation of "landschop" on the coasts of the North Sea, they discover a medieval cultural closeness that other scholars have only glimpsed,[5] one also involving the sophistication of medieval coastal agricultural improvement and the immigration of Frisians into low-lying coastal England.[6] West Frisian proves astoundingly rich in ancient terms still known to farmers and others who work with the soil there but unknown to the Dutch living in Frisia and even to Frisian professionals—yet sometimes known to English farmers.[7] Around 1600, literate Englishmen began writing the word as **landskip** or **landskep** to identify paintings representing views across water toward land. Not for decades did it designate scenery pleasing to the eye: first it denoted informational elevations of harbor topography and similar terrain. Late nineteenth-century German geographers dragged it (and its French near-synonyms) into a conceptual (chiefly political) framework they designated **landschaft**, something still skewing contemporary scholarly understanding of the term "landscape." But what children make on the wet sand is the essence of what West Frisians knew as making land, something for which they had a precise vocabulary.

Nomenclature matters, especially on the beach. **Landschap**, the modern Dutch word that lexicographers assert translates as the English "landscape," seems to have evolved from **landschop**. At its seaward edge, "landschop" edges into **shelf** or **shelp**, submerged land akin to that made by children shoveling in the thinnest shallows.[8] Lexicographers cannot explain the seeming random variation between **p** and **f** in early English, but they know that by the middle of the sixteenth century **shelf** designated sandbanks in the sea and in rivers that make water shallow and difficult, sometimes dangerous, to navigate: as Milton knew in 1634, "tawny sands and shelves" were exposed at low tide.[9] **Shelp** served the same purpose as early as 1430, but somehow also designated plantations of oysters and other shellfish: some writers used **scalp** and **skap** in place of "shelp," suggesting that pronunciation differences indicate different root words. **Shelve** remains a British dialect term designating the tipping of a tip cart, something resembling the tipping of oyster shells into the water above beds, to increase spawn survival.[10]

Lexicographers wonder at the origin of "shelve" as a standard English verb. They suspect it derives from the West Frisian **skelf**, an adjective meaning something not quite level or straight: "the land shelves" and similar phrases echo old nuances. **Shelving** produces potential impediments to navigation, but oysters, mussels, and other shellfish are also **shelf fish** (**shellfish** is a term that rewards dredging up), living on shelves sometimes made and typically maintained by fishermen who own, or own the rights to use, the undersea land they shape, the only truly submarine real estate.[11] "Shelf" translates into Dutch as **schap**.

Especially in law, and particularly in the English common law defining a man's house as his castle, old real

estate terminology—even the term **real estate** itself—
endures unchanged century after century, recorded in deeds
and other documents preserved in castles and ordinary
county courthouses.[12] **Embankment** and **warping**, two
coastal words, remain significant but subtle, tripping unwary
attorneys and bedeviling any meditative reader of old deeds.
Encyclopedias once defined such words in multipage articles. Rees's *Cyclopaedia: or, Universal Dictionary*, the forty-
one-volume, late eighteenth-century Scottish competitor of
the *Britannica*, revised at the beginning of the nineteenth
century in an American edition, defines **warping** alone in
six closely argued pages. **Embanking** meant raising dikes to
keep out the sea or rivers, what Rees understood as sophisticated work; warping out land meant diking and draining
fens, saltmarsh, and flats for agricultural use by extending
dikes bowed seaward, eventually into the sea, making land
from sea bottom, bailing it out, all activity often accomplished in England by Dutch experts.[13] **Warp** now designates a curve in wood usually caused by damp, but once it
also meant the intermittent controlled flooding of warped
land, skelf land, what the Dutch call **polder**, to bring in thin
layers of mud deemed useful as fertilizer. "Warp" designates
too the heavy lines holding ships to pilings and anchors: on
windless days seamen warped sailing ships seaward from
piers, winching them from one piling or anchor to another.
Determined engineers and farmers warped out land but kept
it slightly skelf, so that seepage would drain into the ditches
pumped constantly by windmills. They warped in fertilizer,
minding dikes and gutters and sluice gates, and worrying
constantly about the depredations of great storms and

burrowing animals, rats and moles especially.[14] Words matter to anyone looking competently at landscape, especially at dry land once tidal. Especially today.

The sly and the clever creatively misuse words and torture "landscape" in particular. **Cityscape**, **townscape**, **streetscape**, **brainscape**, **hairscape**, **cloudscape**, **airscape**, **hardscape**, **bedscape**, and other nonce words exist because "landscape" is now a promiscuous word indeed. Its progeny confuse anyone looking around thoughtfully, even at the ocean. In art history circles, **seascape** designates a concept and image type older than "landscape," something even young children seem to know when asked which is older, the sea or the land. They look up from their pails and shovels, away from their castles and embankments, walls and gateways, gaze seaward and instinctively know the great age of the sea and the comparative newness of the land. Variable, moody, implacable, unstable, the sea endures beyond shovels and shaping. The built fabric inland from the beach and dunes appears stable, and so beguiles and reassures the thoughtless. It lends itself to advertising hype, to word-making about making and shaping, to expressions like **moral landscape** and **financial landscape**, phrases designating things not subject to sudden sea change.

Its complexity occludes the very words intended to name its components and facilitate understanding, especially the basic, old words children learn before they learn to read.

Often they learn the word **moat** from adults helping them build sand castles. A difficult word, "moat." It vexes lexicographers who suspect its origins in Old French or

Celtic synonyms, **hill**, **bank**, or **dike**. Adults think it means the excavated form filled with water, not the raised berm or verge or rim. At the beach, playing in the sun, children learn about shaping land against the sea, the visual iconography of castles and moats and dikes, and even some of the old words, "moat" included.

In a land-centric culture they learn nothing of approaching the beach from the sea, nothing of what mariners call **sea state**, nothing of the near impossibility of estimating surf height from the sea itself.[15] They learn nothing of estimating distance to horizon, descrying the curve of the horizon, or of looming and other atmospheric phenomena crucial to realizing the world is not flat. They might learn to have fun in boats, but few become intimate with sea language.

Near the coast, approaching land, **making land** as seamen still call it, sailing among sandbanks and other shape-shifting hazards, sixteenth-century North Sea mariners understood "landschop" to mean new-made land warped out into shallows. "Landschop" (or "landschap") entered English as **altumal**. (Derived from the Latin **altum** meaning the deep or the ocean, "altumal" designates the dialect of merchant seamen and shallow-water traders, a sort of mercantile language of the sea, shaping and reshaping coastal dialects.[16] It remains on the marges of lexicography in part because it rarely existed in writing and still retains terms and pronunciations unknown on land. Tackle for example—the blocks, ropes, and cables landsmen refer to as **block-and-tackle** or **fishing tackle**—is still pronounced "tay-kel" by older seamen, a pronunciation accepted as "nautical" by a handful of superb dictionaries.[17]) On the low-lying North Sea coasts, especially among the Frisian Islands and inlets, any landschop might be a pilotage hazard: gales shifted sandbanks erratically, but landsmen warping out land might wreck ships and small craft too, if not directly then by diverting currents which move sandbars. Seamen knew every landschop was important in pilotage, especially in storms when each one served as landmark and as hazard to be avoided.

Approaching low-lying sandy land, then and now, involves great skill. Navigation charts typically have offered only plan views useful to deep-sea shipmasters, who expected to pick up local-knowledge pilots off harbors. Most local or pilotage charts still depict shoals and channels sketched from above, often as approximations. Along sandy coasts, shoals and channels wander annually and sometimes more frequently, outdating most charts. Reckoning position proves perilous, even to local fishermen. Coasts devoid of cliffs and hills, indeed of almost any vertical element, confuse, especially in rain, fog, and dark. By the fifteenth century a few chart makers—and some ship masters sketching their own pilots or rutters—began including sketches of coasts seen in elevation.[18]

Rutter, grounded in the French word **routier**, meaning a guide to the ways, itself grounded in Old French **rote** via the later **route**, is the Frisian, Dutch, and English pronunciation. Away from France, **rut** skewed **routier**. Designating a groove worn by cart wheels or a plowed groove or furrow, the term meant then and still means a fixed practice or way of proceeding intended as safe, intentionally neither boring nor exciting. Along rural reaches of British, American, and Canadian coasts, the active listener still hears fishermen speak of **rutters**, their altumal pronunciation of **rudder**, the swinging, vertical plane that shapes the course of a boat or ship.[19] Approaching a low-lying coast, even for small-craft fishermen intimate with it, means knowing the **rote** of the sea, its roaring soft or loud, still pronounced "rut" in places where "rudder" is "rutter." Sixteenth-century rutters displaced no pilots, but aided shipmasters regularly calling at low-lying, sandy inlets. Warping out land aided the making of rutters because the land behind the dikes, often land below sea level, required continuous pumping into channels sometimes navigable by small coasting vessels.

Windmills pumped so long as the wind revolved their sails. Netherlands landsmen knew them as icons of triumph, machines keeping salt water at bay, constantly bailing, markers of territory won from the sea by people restless under Spanish sovereignty. From the building of the first windmill late in the sixteenth century, mariners knew them too as position indicators, especially the grain-milling ones sited atop great dunes. Often sited in pairs and clusters, the vertical forms served as critical seamarks. They became the signature structures of Frisia, Holland, and adjacent low-lying provinces, and in time the signature structures of an independent country, the Netherlands.

Today the pinwheels fluttering atop sand castles announce something forgotten by almost everyone. To the Frisians and Hollanders, then to the Dutch, windmills substituted for castles, rising from low-lying, sandy coasts and heralding the technical expertise, design, and political stability shaping the warping out of land, the making of landschop, the rise of the Dutch republic. Adults buy children pinwheels because pinwheels somehow belong at the beach. They harness wind energy purely for pleasure but they do harness it, alerting smart children to environmental forces shaping sand castles and whatever else people build and sometimes blowing sand into ridges and even dunes. Sandcastles and pinwheels illustrate the political and technical power implicit in the making and maintenance of landscape.

On the summer beach glistens the essential landscape, something any observant, thoughtful individual might ponder. He or she might consider the role of natural forces, the fall of light, the roles of clouds; how blowing sand becomes nuisance, then obnoxious as the wind rises. Maybe the observer wonders about the loss of beach nomenclature in an era devoted to beach recreation and resorts, unmissed terms like **guzzle** and **shingle** enabling two people to talk precisely about the ripples in sand exposed at low tide.[20] Or the meditative watcher might wonder at legal concepts, the marge where real estate and the law of the land meet ownerless sea and nautical or admiralty law, where assault-and-battery becomes mutiny. Connected experimenters might carry precious electronic gadgets into the shallows, scrutinizing GPS screens as these shift from map to chart display. More traditional scrutinizers might ponder the distinctions separating landscape imagery, especially painting and photography, from seascapes and marines. Jan van Goyen's seventeenth-century *A Windmill by a River* depicts a grain mill atop a great dune overlooking landschop and sea, but Jacob van Ruisdael's near-contemporaneous *Stormy Sea* depicts a fishing boat desperately aiming for the channel between two parallel rows of pilings guarding a harbor entrance. Most museumgoers viewing the two mid-seventeenth-century Netherlandish paintings easily call the first a "landscape" but hesitate when labeling the second.[21] The former has lots of land and little sea, the second much wild ocean but only two rows of pilings protecting a sandy channel from silting, a vertical daymark, a sailing vessel in peril, and two men standing atop one groin running seaward from sand. Geographers, oceanographers, mariners, and aficionados of pillar mills might see the paintings differently from art history professors and their students, and all experts advance their views ceaselessly, using "landscape" carelessly or in arcane, vested-interest ways which put off inquirers intrigued by larger wholes.

Not every day at the beach shimmers in sunlit museum stillness. Fog changes everything. Fog "comes in" without help from the wind. It keeps vacationers indoors, delays automobile traffic and wrecks airline schedules, misleads walkers (especially at night), plays tricks with sound. Fog changes everything, changes everything viscerally. To know fog at the beach is to know the second cousin of undertow and of great gales and hurricanes alongshore.

In great storms the determined watcher learns that submarine terrain shapes sand and dunes and even built form inland. A mile or more offshore some ledges break only in century storms: far submerged even at low tide, they reveal themselves when the deepest wave troughs hit them, making surf explode above. As such ledges **break**—the alongshore

word usually designates a fish leaping clear of the water—
they break the great rollers which break again on shallow
ledges closer inshore. In the aftermath of great storms the
observer sees some houses undamaged while those around
them are destroyed. Given the identical elevation above and
distance from the ordinary tidemark, the pattern puzzles.
But the standing houses remain because they are inshore of
the deep ledges, within cones of protection; often they are
antique, built according to ancient knowledge about the
century storms which strike roughly every hundred years,
wilderness events revealing ledges that protect built form.[22]
Storms remind every observer that natural forces impact
what people build. Sometimes storms send observers to shelter, dry clothes, hot coffee, and books about landscape
(maybe this one).

In summer sunshine, children and adults ignore books
and stand to admire creations shaped from sand. From above
they look over land walled against the sea. Such **uitgestrektheid land**, "land that is overlooked," means in early Dutch
something other than valley land seen from a mountaintop. It
means land embanked against the sea, shoveled up in shelves,
drained, flat, continually pumped; land easily looked across
from the made high ground, the tops of dikes, land taken in
with a single long glance often because it seems nearly fea-
tureless, punctuated with few if any vertical elements.[23]

Here follows then an introduction to landscape for the
individual inquirer who inquires directly before exploring the
vast, sometimes fog-bound literature on a well-nigh ubiquitous subject. Scholars and other experts, some self-announced,
use "landscape" as subtly or carelessly or invidiously as

advertisers and entertainment-industry writers, as desperately as deadline-struck journalists use it. Theoretical concepts and advertising and marketing ploys work best on people who fail to explore landscape firsthand.

Experienced beachgoers scoop a shallow hole in the sand before sitting. A little ergonomic excavation makes sitting easy on the back. After they depart, the barefoot inquirer walking along a deserted beach spies the holes and footprints and realizes what Robinson Crusoe knew, that a footprint means a temporary presence, a hole means a savvy sitter. The holes say a bit more, that someone stopped and shaped and then abandoned the depression to wind and tide. No crumbling sandcastles, no discarded pinwheel, nothing but depressions made by feet and hands ... has the inquirer found an abandoned landscape? Well ... no.

Start then with looking around.

Snow falling at end of day on unfamiliar back roads makes the long-distance traveler suddenly wary of nightfall, gas gauge and 4WD buttons, GPS vagaries and abandoned motels, and all the occluded return of wilderness. JRS

1 Making

Individuals conjure landscape individually. Each inquirer realizes something unique in the concatenation of shapes and forms and spaces and colors and textures ahead or around. Someone tall has a longer view than someone short: someone with 20/5 vision may scrutinize the far distance more acutely than someone who routinely focuses on the middle ground. Such distinctions lie in the realm of perception studies. Childhood experience, formal education, occupational training, and nuanced unknowns all likewise contribute to the individual making of peculiar landscape. Scholars sometimes attempt to exorcise individual conjuring by rationalizing the conceptualization of landscape according to favorite ideologies or conceptual frameworks or by writing software bereft of human nature. Landscape mocks scholars. Groups of people share certain general angles of vision and agree on certain rough-hewn simplicities, but landscape perception is peculiar to each inquirer. Discovering how a close friend understands landscape proves

awkward and often tedious: words occlude perceptions.
Discovering how those now dead perceived landscape
proves wearying but intermittently enlightening.

With care, inquirers can understand the landscape con-
jurings of others, but only rarely can they escape, even
momentarily, the contemporary mindset.

At sea in a small, traditionally built sailing boat, the amateur mariner eschewing engine, charts, and electronic gadgetry edges into a near-timeless experience. The wind and
sea, rain and fog remain constants from ages before.
Approaching the land, perhaps especially in foul weather
where the coast is unmarked, challenges and instructs. The
mariner holds a clenched fist straight out, against the land:
across the knuckles measures nine degrees, three between
each knuckle, a fifth of the total marked by the clenched fist
with thumb extended.[1] Using such ancient techniques facilitates making a landfall, closing the land from open sea, estimating distance made good. Much of the process involved
for centuries—and still involves for determined aficionados
of traditional pilotage—the most intense imaginable attention to currents, tides, wind, and sea state.[2] From seaward,
for example, the height of surf on beaches proves almost
impossible to reckon, and landing through combers may
mean calamity.[3] Making a harbor entrance, even entering a
great bay during storms, means avoiding hazards, currents
colliding in tide races, then the rocks, ledges, and sandbars
that are somehow neither sea nor land which invest shoal
water with destruction and sudden death, which correctly
frighten steamship masters who take aboard local-knowledge
pilots before approaching large, well-marked ports. "Venture

just two miles offshore and the land will start slipping into the sea, for that is how close the horizon appears when viewed from a small boat," muses Roger Barnes in *The Dinghy Cruising Companion.* "The sea still offers the promise of freedom and escape to anyone with the confidence to venture out upon it."[4] But it also twists contemporary mass-media understanding of safety and comfort, self-reliance and honed physical skill. It twists too landlubber complacency.

"*Avel Dro* is sailing at the limit of what she can safely handle, but the danger adds to the stark beauty of the scene," Barnes writes of nearing the entrance to Lorient in his fifteen-foot sailing dinghy, caught in rising wind and sea. "I am sweeping over a landscape of blue rolling hills, shimmering in the sunlight, ever moving, ever changing, and awesome in their power. It is breathtakingly spectacular. ... There is breaking water on a raft of black rocks close to leeward of us and a confused mass of lateral marks fills the channel ahead."[5] Modern mindset and modern foul-weather attire notwithstanding, Barnes experiences the age-old experience of the sea as landscape, still safe at the moment for his tiny boat crossing from England to France, and the ledges and channels and land as wilderness which wreck with a touch. Then he enters the lee of a point and old fort, the seas and wind drop, and he understands all astern as wilderness and all ahead as landscape, ordered, civil, welcoming, safe harbor, graced with inns and cafés.

Against "a long low yellow coast of sand dunes, apparently devoid of any habitation," Frank Mulville lost his big sailboat in the Frisian Islands on the sandbar shelves of landschop. "The mist had lifted a little and we could just see the

outline of the shore on our starboard side," he recalled of the
tide and stiff breeze driving *Transcur* at six knots. Then he
and his wife and young children heard a roaring like that of
a railroad train, the steep seas became surf, and in the gathering mist the boat struck sand, the first roller crashed over
it, smashing into its cabin and turning the hull broadside,
and the next loomed close. "I saw this wave out of the corner
of my eye, the vicious curving crest, coloured a light brown
by tiny suspended particles of sand, seemed to hover for an
instant high up above *Transcur*'s stern and then quite deliberately, it moved in like a great foaming hound converging
for the kill." Chaos triumphed. Mulville recounts trying to
lash the tiller before the seas tore off the rudder. "I fought
with it as if it were a ferocious animal and strove to get it
amidships so that I could fasten the tiller lines round it, but
with the strength of a tiger it wrenched itself from side to
side in fury."[6] Malevolence and wild-animal similes shape
his account because all forces arrayed against his family
seemed sentient, wicked. The vast low-tide sandbanks
offered no safety. Nor did the low-lying, made land beyond.

In a small open boat, the traditionalist encounters what
deep-sea mariners find, emotions which rise with inchoate
sensory realization. "Breathless it was, in spite of the cold,
and there was that indescribable feeling of menace, always
present before a violent storm; I felt it all around me,"
remembered Elis Karlsson of the minutes before his steamship slammed into rocks. "This would be the moment, on
board a sailing-ship, to check up on everything and prepare
the ship for the onslaught." But the master and mates relied
completely on the local-knowledge pilot, reassured that "a

man is in charge who knows the land and the shoals around him."[7] In stiffening wind and gathering dusk Karlsson could not escape the feeling of menace. Soon he was aboard a lifeboat, soaked, and slowly freezing to death while struggling to avoid surf-wrapped hazards. The traditionalist amateur finds alongshore fright far more frequently than deep-sea professionals, and sometimes, especially at night, learns that similes and emotions prove as timeless as the eldritch inshore pilotage terror generating feelings of menace and dread.[8] But typically the traditionalist wears up-to-date foul-weather gear which skews traditional experience, if only a little, and always he carries the modern mindset, something less easy to discard when swimming.

Against such deep-past, traditional limicole effort buzzes the contemporary one of the amateur airplane pilot and the far noisier one of the airliner passenger.

Manned flight dates to 1783, when the Montgolfier brothers sent aloft a basket slung beneath a great balloon. The view from above, at first described simply as the longed-for bird's-eye view, proved both vertical and oblique: once aloft, the balloons required little attention, and aeronauts and their passengers looked down and around freely. Throughout the first half of the nineteenth century, balloons drifted from scientific instruments to the playthings of the wealthy, carried military observers linked by telegraph wires in the Civil War, and segued into entertainment vehicles.[9] After 1870, thousands of Americans rode in balloons tethered to winches fixed in county fairground centers; hundreds of others, all lucky winners of raffles, enjoyed flying free, often alone.[10]

Lizzie Ihling went aloft alone over Pennsylvania in October 1876 on a rainy day, seeing momentarily "towns and villages" and then nothing but "sulky-black" heavy overcast which became "a milk-white vapor" once it enveloped her. "Presently I heard quite distinctly the tinkling of a cow-bell, and, supposing I had crossed over to Bald Eagle Valley, I came down gradually," opening the valve according to direction. "There was a mountain and a valley in the cloud surface" and she descended beneath the clouds, recognized a farm beneath her, and after passing low over a graveyard, landed where she had hoped. She found the flight "wholly novel and sublime, as it was my first experience." Readers of the weekly newspaper learned that she felt no fear. She controlled the balloon, knelt fascinated in the basket, and for the first time in her life recognized farm fields as more suitable for landing than woods and graveyards.[11]

In the 1890s, as bicycling replaced canoeing as the premier national recreation, many air-fascinated American writers assumed ballooning and motorized ballooning (and perhaps gliding) would soon eclipse cycling. *St. Nicholas* and other children's magazines emphasized that children would soon fly on their own. In "Young Crusoes of the Sky," F. Lovell Coombs imagined the adventures of three young boys accidentally adrift in a balloon and addressed their perception of what lay under them: "In eager, silent wonder the three boys saw the white floor of mist roll from beneath them and a great map open out to view. For a space the shadow of the clouds continued to obscure the landscape, then it too swept on, and a great checker-board of green and yellow, barred with lanes of white, lay spread out before them." The boys descry towns, wonder at "a flattened glassy ribbon wriggl[ing] across the landscape," and puzzle at the saucer-like form of the earth spread beneath and around them: not flat, sort of a shallow soup plate, the shape seems to contain the gridded Midwest spectacle.[12] Coombs made clear that the boys were part of the generation born to see landscape through clouds, to wonder at large-scale spatial and atmospheric distortion, and to fly in silence with the leisure to look and think.

Adults and some teenagers had begun flying under large, tethered kites. In an 1897 article in *Century Magazine*, Hugh D. Wise, an American army officer, explained how to build and use kites framed with metal tubes and described the sensation as "a gentle swaying and lifting not unlike the motion of a swing," though he dismissed the potential of kite flight as compared to everyday flying in tethered balloons.[13] But Wise understood the proliferation of bicycle industry steel tubes and the airward predilection of teenage boys. He thought flying under kites above housetops was attainable by the young, correctly modern, and likely to encourage aerial engineering.

In the same issue of *Century Magazine*, William A. Eddy recounted his efforts to send cameras aloft on kites. At the close of the nineteenth century Americans had become used to professional balloon-borne photography even if the photographs and stereographs retailed under the term "bird's-eye views." Sending up heavy, glass-plate-negative cameras required large kites, strong lines, and stiff breezes: experimenters and hobbyists first used secondary lines to trip shutters, then replaced lines likely to snag with slow-burning firecracker fuse.[14] Once adults and children began to own inexpensive, lightweight Eastman Kodak Company box cameras, however, amateur engineering and children's magazines emphasized ways to send aloft the cardboard Brownie cameras able to photograph at three to five hundred feet. Everywhere in rural America families treasure fading snapshots made high above farms by kites controlled by late-nineteenth-century children standing far below and hoping for perfect exposures.[15]

Just before the Wright brothers flew their engine-powered aircraft at Kitty Hawk blossomed a still unstudied national experiment with amateur flying, airborne photography, and aerial landscape analysis. A few teenage boys built one-person dirigibles, powered them with crude propellers turned by bicycle cranks, and made short flights over their neighborhoods. The hydrogen-filled, coated muslin gas bags offered just enough lift, and the large rudders, made of muslin stretched over bamboo frames, offered just enough steerageway, at least in calms. If the teenage boys had time to look down, wonder, and perhaps photograph, few records remain. At the close of the nineteenth century, flying had morphed into something finicky, an enterprise requiring continuous sustained control of fragile aircraft. Men and boys built gliders, lay beneath them, and coasted down snow-covered hills until the airfoils lifted them from careening sleds. Now and then the lucky glided over a valley, caught a thermal rising from a factory smokestack, and enjoyed a long if teeth-gritting ride. None of the glider pilots made photographs.[16] Flying—and landing—preoccupied them. It preoccupied less the pilots of engine-driven dirigibles.

Once having gained a bit of altitude, dirigibles might be slowed or stopped, made to hover or allowed to drift. One-to three-person dirigibles enabled a bit of downward musing and photography jarred by engine vibration. But once engines stopped, flight became as silent as ballooning: only while under way did rigging whistle in the wind the way sailing-ship rigging (and kite strings) whistle.[17] Until about 1940 rigid dirigibles, called **zeppelins** after their German inventor, offered passengers, especially women and girls, not only engine-powered flight but intermittent freedom from engine noise. Dirigibles made stable platforms for photography, and after the 1929 invention of the Leica 35mm camera, opening windows allowed passengers to lean out, focus, and photograph. In the 1930s zeppelins carried passengers almost accident-free across the Atlantic. The so-called Zeppelin Ferry between Berlin and New York introduced hundreds of well-to-do passengers to the sheer joy of flying low over parts of Europe and then south along the coast of Maine to Lakehurst in New Jersey. Occasionally, in gentle airs and when the light proved photogenic, zeppelin captains flew close and slowly over North Atlantic icebergs, urging passengers to open windows, lean forward, gaze, and make photographs. When the *Hindenburg* exploded in New Jersey in 1937, popular fascination with airships began eroding. By 1940 nascent airlines offered long flights across the British Empire and to other nations using gigantic flying boats that landed on water in Africa and elsewhere. For a brief moment, water became airstrip.

Within ten years of its invention, the Wright brothers' engine-driven aircraft had been co-opted for military use and by a near-fanatic emphasis on speed.[18] Piloting the first airplanes meant confronting innate instability, damage caused by rough landings, and frequent engine failure, and often all three combined in emergency landings. In-flight battle damage, especially fire, forced landings throughout World War I and forever shaped the attitude and training of pilots, particularly postwar amateurs flying military-surplus small planes. "For the first time, I looked at the country below the way the older pilots were always telling us young ones to look: always looking for a possible landing place, all the way cross-country," recalled Wolfgang Langewiesche in his 1939 *I'll Take the High Road*, "picking this cow pasture, that hay field, that broad highway, much as a man might walk across a stream and pick his stepping stones." More than most flyers, he logged what he saw, "just ordinary Middle West," with railroad tracks, a river, checkerboard expanses of fields, buzzing over "a house, and its backyard, and a woman hanging up the wash, and then contemptuously across the corner of a small town," worrying (but not a lot) about his feelings of superiority, and far more about navigation, fuel supply, and finding a place to light upon if the engine sputtered.[19]

Zeppelin passengers wrote often about landscape, but airplane pilots and passengers did so far less frequently. Anne Morrow Lindbergh proved an exception. Her *North to the Orient*, recounting flights made in 1931, enumerated much about which her celebrity aviator husband said nothing.[20] For the first time she flew from Washington, D.C., to North Haven in Maine. She missed the gradations in scene and time provided by the passenger train and steamer and some of her favorite way points, and decided that "the familiar landmarks below me had no reality," that her body speeded along ahead of her mind, in a lack of synchronization robbing her "of the realization of life and therefore much of its joy." In the two-seater pontoon plane (its shape presaging that of World War II fighters) and afterward, Lindbergh learned to "sit quite still and let the roar of the engine cover me like music," to look out and see "a wooded hill like moss, soft gray moss to crush in one's hands" and "the shadow of a single elm, flat on the ground, like a pressed fern," the sides of houses in the morning sun, "bright rectangles and squares, like the facets of cut stones."[21] One of the first passengers to accustom herself to international air travel, the view of harbors and lakes from a fast-descending float plane, and the gradually increasing altitude of long-haul flight, Lindbergh pondered the contempt Langewiesche shrugged off. A decade later Beryl Markham related near-identical concerns in *West with the Night*, but she mused more precisely on the way the speeding airplane swept her past incongruities in the landscape, realization dawning perhaps twenty miles further on.[22] Pilots had too much to do to ponder the landscape below: "look around idly, and before you knew it, you were 'messed up,'" Langewiesche concluded.[23] In 1948 Lindbergh flew to Europe as an airliner passenger. She condemned the American passengers as detached, able to observe but feel nothing about the landscapes below, "comfortable, well-fed, aloof, and superior." She condemned especially "the terrible thing—the curious illusion of superiority bred by height, the illusion of being a god." Airliner travel produced an "illusion of terrible power."[24] It made landscape mere show—or target.

In the 1920s, mass-circulation and specialist magazines alike championed the personal or family flying machine always just over the horizon, the thing that would speed commuting, eliminate traffic jams, and whisk the family to the beach—the amphibious car, perhaps, nimble on the highway and in the air.[25] Henry Ford took up the challenge, then canceled his Sky Car, what hopefuls called "the flying flivver," at the end of the decade after it killed a friend.[26] The Los Angeles Public Schools operated an aerial classroom by 1927, flying children (properly seated at desks) over the sprawling city as part of its geography curriculum. But the children did not fly on their own.[27] In 1930 readers of *Parents' Magazine* learned that many young teenage boys, bored with automobiles, hung around simple airfields and learned to fly almost intuitively: perhaps they heralded a post-automobile age, an age of males aloft.[28] In the Depression the amphibious-car dream and airborne classroom faded despite half-hearted government support, and while reborn in World War II, they disappeared again in the early 1950s. A handful of flying cars failed the rough-landing test or proved hopelessly uncomfortable on the road. Despite the fad of 1960s kit-built, one-person helicopters (nerve-wracking to fly) and subsequent hang-gliding and ultralight fads, children do not yet fly simple, helium-lifted, bicycle-powered dirigibles above neighborhood landscape.[29] The continuous attention needed to fly what aficionados call "kites" keeps young children from even trying hang-gliding or its motorized cousin: teenagers do not build gliders and seek thermals, as they most certainly did until about 1942.[30] Hobbyists know that looking closely at landscape from a hang glider, let alone making photographs, proves unwise.[31] As Jennifer Van Vleck demonstrates in *Empire of the Air: Aviation and the American Ascendancy*, military technology and deep-pocket capitalism repeatedly overwhelmed personal-flight optimism and experiment.

Riding a bicycle is unforgettable. So is flying. But bicycling empowers little children on first two-wheelers and offers older children and adults intimate short-range exploration of local worlds. Flight remains fundamentally different and even its early history (and hopes) vague. Only a handful of boys flew over their homes and neighborhoods circa 1900, pedaling unwieldy science-project airships, and remarkably few adults hang-glide or fly ultralights today. But when the airliner leaves the runway or descends at the end of the flight, children especially stare downward, faces against too-small windows. Whatever it is they notice and feel today, the aerial view transformed all perception of landscape and landscape history, landscape studies, landscape design too, and it forever altered landscape drawing, painting, and photography. Early amateur flying gets too little attention from walkers and bicyclists and motorists. An aerial image has no foreground objects, except perhaps a cloud or a wing strut.[32] The traditional mariner aboard a restored or replica small boat may try to imagine himself back in time, but no aviator can imagine herself aloft before 1903—or perhaps 1783.

Flight illustrates how different contemporary landscape conjuring is from that of a century or two past. It rams home the impossibility of knowing much at all about how earlier generations understood the landscapes they created or found or abandoned. Contemporary inquirers cannot shake airborne perception. Indeed, flight rams home the changes wrought in the 1930s, as float planes penetrated the Canadian north and flight transformed—forever—the viewpoint of experienced canoeist-cartographers.[33] The Byzantines "could imagine how God looked down from on high on the fields, on the towns, and on the gilded domes of the churches," remarks Karel Tomeï in *De bovenkant van Nederland: Holland from the Top*, a collection of aerial images of landscape. They understood their environs, even their empire, he asserts, as an imperfect mirror of Heaven. "In our individualist era, the airborne camera restores awareness of the connectedness of place. Once you look at the world from high up in the air, you see that there is more unity in all that thrashing around to create our own individual heavens than you thought," he cautions, reminding readers that older religious worldviews illuminate the contemporary illusion of superiority, of being God-like, that Lindbergh feared.[34] In the end, however, airborne photography produces images dependent on lens type. Flying produces unnerving reflections on ground and ocean travel, let alone on fairies and Peter Pan. However one conceives of European exploration and imperialism, it proceeded by land and by sea. And nowhere did explorers meet people who could fly.

After about 1400, European explorers arrived at many places hitherto beyond their knowledge, but most proved inhabited. People lived almost everywhere the explorers ventured, but no European "discoverers" expressed surprise at

finding them. "The nearly universal distribution of human-
ity, which so exceeded the geographical range of any other
mammal, never drew their attention," argues Clive Gamble
in *Timewalkers: The Prehistory of Global Colonization*. Only
recently have archaeologists and anthropologists traced the
outlines of prehistoric movement, especially across oceans,
for example finding that Indonesians settled Madagascar
from the east and that other seafarers settled all of the Pacific
islands from the west. Gamble emphasizes that "in both
cases colonization was highly focused and directed, firmly
rooted in the ideology of the homeland society, and due neither to *chance drift* nor a simple matter of *enough time*, as is
argued for the dispersal of animals and plants." Out of
Africa came pioneers. Over millennia their descendants settled almost everywhere. Some islands truly deserved the
label "deserted"—Bermuda, Ascension, St. Helena, the
Galapagos, among a handful of others—but many bereft of
people proved only vacant: Christmas, Norfolk, and Pitcairn
all boast evidence of prehistoric settlement abandoned
before European contact. "We investigate landscapes expect-
ing to find prehistoric occupation even though the area may
be uninhabited today," Gamble states of his research in
southwest Tasmania, in a rocky wilderness reserve. "This is
difficult country where it can take a day to walk a kilometer.
Helicopters have changed that, but no one had been to this
valley with its small cave for over 12,000 years."[35] Gamble
and his colleagues can learn a bit from excavating the floor
of the cave but cannot hope to understand how its occupants conjured a landscape: scholars arriving in helicopters

can imagine only so much, their imaginations already permanently twisted by aerial transit.

Nonetheless, archaeologists and other inquirers work
heartened by the simple truth expressed by Giambattista
Vico in 1725: people like ourselves made the past. "We can
know the world of the past because that world was the product of *Homo faber*—man the maker," argues D. Bruce Dickson in *The Dawn of Belief: Religion in the Upper Paleolithic of
Southwestern Europe*. Being makers ourselves enables us to
understand our forebears: "This is certainly true of their
technology and subsistence practices and is perhaps equally
true of their religion." Dickson imagines an archaeologist of
the distant future attempting to study Christianity while
lacking anything written. The inquirer would note the ori-
entation of church buildings, the lack of items buried with
the dead, the way towns and cities seem gathered to churches
at their centers, the immense stables, granaries, workshops,
and other structures dovetailed into the chapels of medieval
monastic establishments. "From the very beginning of this
study, the archaeologist would no doubt be aware of the
extra-European origins of early Christianity," Dickson
notes, and while much would be occluded (the lives of the
saints, the Inquisition, the beginnings of the Reformation),
Christian art and architecture would reveal much, especially
the way icons suggest a greater visual focus in worship east
of Rome. While da Vinci's *Last Supper* might strike an Australian aborigine as depicting a dinner, Dickson demonstrates how much artifacts reveal of issues beyond
subsistence. And he argues incisively that "upper Paleolithic
peoples made an important spatial distinction between

'living space,' in the light and above ground where their everyday activities took place, and 'ceremonial space,' in the dark galleries below the earth's surface where extraordinary actions took place."[36]

Often almost inaccessible (today to reach one gallery an inquirer "must cross two underground lakes by boat and then scale a 131-foot cliff wall"), this subterranean location suggests that much of the art existed for only a few. At other sites, however, relatively easy accessibility suggests much wider participation. "The interiors of the great caverns of southwestern Europe may have formed an internal frontier for the people of the Upper Paleolithic, a frontier which expanded only gradually over the generations" as people conquered darkness "on both technical and emotional planes," Dickson argues, in a way presaging how their descendants mastered the night (more or less) via electricity. He emphasizes that in dark churches the icons of Eastern Orthodox Christianity prove strikingly powerful when surrounded in candlelight: "they shimmer and seem to float above the protean sea of light created by banks of candles gleaming beneath them." An ordinary museum display case breaks their religious spell.[37] Vico would find the early humans much like ourselves, preferring daylight, nocturnal only by culture, still enamored of fire, fireworks, LEDs, and glowing screens.[38] Dickson and other archaeologists move painstakingly by looking closely: they have no one to ask and often only vestigial and shattered clues.

Myth, religious scripture, and the roots of language—especially in place names and perhaps especially in place names properly pronounced—combine now to produce studies of landscapes far distant in time. In *The Destruction of Sodom, Gomorrah, and Jericho: Geological, Climatological, and Archaeological Background*, David Neev (a geologist) and K. O. Emery (an oceanographer) analyze Old Testament accounts of urban destruction. Working among extant structures about ten thousand years old (at the end of the era Dickson examines), and struggling to pinpoint the actual locales of places mentioned in the Bible (finding that the pillar of salt into which Lot's wife turned is so variously identified that Lot might well have had a harem), they focus on remnant evidence of catastrophe. While the precise site of Sodom city remains unknown, the presence of ozokerite oil seeping from the base of a nearby sandstone escarpment provides one explanation for the post-earthquake (or other rupture) smoke, fire, and stench Scripture records. Part of their work revolves around variant meanings of the ancient Hebrew word **kittor**, which designates a stream of water but can mean a pillar of smoke (as it does in Genesis 19:28) and might just as well have designated a stream of burning, high-sulfur, hydrogen-sulfide-laced asphalt, making smoke visible twenty miles off.[39] Knowing any holy writing (and perhaps knowing modern exegesis as well) opens portals not only on palimpsest landscapes but on unchanged behavior of winds.

In 1954, yachtsman Charles Violet knew that scholars understand Tarshish as the Old Testament name for Sardinia. In a driving gale near the island, he thought of Psalm 48, "Thou breakest the ships of Tarshish with an east wind."[40] The verse matters still in part because the east wind sometimes rages in the same place. Archaeologists (and other experts) thus piece together the tiniest of fragments and hints into filmy and firm constructs, often using large-scale aerial photography (as do Neeve and Emery) to advance their efforts in understanding seafarers and other pioneers who could only imagine flight.

Piecing together works well for any inquirer into landscape. Curiosity and observation shape inquiry. Skill improves with practice. Even at night.

Far from cities, starlight illuminates moonless, cloudless nights well enough that cautious travelers may walk freely. Small-boat mariners soon grow acquainted with starlit dark, but tourists rarely note that skiffs and aircraft carriers carry only red and green navigation lights announcing their presence. Vessels carry no headlights. In mid-ocean and deserts, clear night sky reveals the Milky Way and thousands of stars no longer visible in cities and suburbs: if nothing else, the array makes celestial navigation straightforward. But understanding landscape after dark away from artificial illumination involves arcane techniques. Looking ever so slightly away from what one descries surprises in its efficiency: rods and cones are not evenly distributed in the human eye. Vinson Brown's *Reading the Outdoors at Night* remains the best guide to nocturnal overland exploration. Away from streetlights, with flashlight and cell phone screen gone dead, the benighted walker employs its techniques to get along and—perhaps—ponder the long history of landscape at night.

"Watergate Row was a dim, mysterious place after dark, lit only by infrequent flickering gas lamps," recalls L. T. C. Rolt of an English cathedral-town alley at Christmas in 1914. In falling snow his family delighted in the near-total darkness and shards of artificial light reflected from drifted whiteness. The shuttered shops "showed chinks of light" too, and the boy walked attentively. Occasionally "the mouth of a narrow alley, dark as midnight and leading who knows where, opens up between them," and Rolt remembers thinking of the candlelit choir of the cathedral in which he had been singing carols a few minutes earlier. The dark and the contrast of the "whiteness of the snow" and the slivers of artificial, flickering light "combined to induce a receptive mood in which my recollection of this dim tunnel of Watergate Row was registered and stored away in some most profound level of conscious memory. I could not have said why." Rolt catches something of the prehistoric cave lit by fire, of the icon surrounded by candlelight.[41]

In his massive *Landscape Trilogy*, he tries repeatedly to distinguish what the adult "must needs rationalize and formulate" from that which "the child grasped intuitively." Somehow, perhaps due to his anticipation of Christmas magic, he "perceived then an embodiment of the continuing life of an ancient city, labyrinthine, dark, mysterious yet not sinister but intensely human." His nighttime experience shaped Rolt's lifetime of landscape analysis, his spearheading the campaign to preserve and restore most of Britain's eighteenth-century canal system, and his success as an antiquarian. What modern city, he asked, "could make such an impression upon a child?"[42] Rolt noticed and internalized long before he analyzed. Never did he lose his thoughtfulness about the ways children perceive landscape and especially the dark, perhaps especially when Christmas excitement and lights shape perception. Never did he lose sight of something else: in Watergate Row, in near darkness, he walked in safety.

Ambivalence about darkness, especially urban darkness, shapes all contemporary understanding of nighttime landscape. City dwellers think streetlights, foyer lights, parking lot lights, and motion-detecting lights deflect criminals. That such lights make getting about easier (even for criminals) is only afterthought. Just after sundown many urban motorists forget to turn on headlights because highways and streets are so well illuminated that vehicle lights seem superfluous. Automobile headlights endure from the era when overcast skies prompted nightwalkers, especially away from gaslit city centers, to carry lanterns. Horseless-carriage manufacturers knew that suburbanites and country families would prove their chief market (both lived away from public transit systems) and borrowed railroad technology. Even today railroad companies do not light their rights of way: locomotives carry multiple, blinding headlights. A railroad track at night remains one of the darkest ribbons in the modern world, not only in wilderness areas but everywhere else, in farmland and near urban terminals. Here and there blazes a signal, its colored light reflecting along parallel gleams of polished steel, but otherwise the right of way is dark. The locomotive headlight illuminates the way ahead, what the engineer stares at so intently, but it continuously warns of what the whistle and bell only intermittently announce: a train is coming.[43] That train endangers trespassers in its way, but at least it announces its coming. On a dark street the honest walker might encounter criminals cloaked by the dark.

Centuries-old law reinforces age-old fear of the dark. Laws provide harsher penalties for breaking and entering by night than for burglary by day, just as they punish masked robbers more harshly than those who show their faces. Darkness and masks occlude, and the contemporary jury finds itself flung backward into far older concerns. Operating a motor vehicle without lights is a crime, but walking in rural areas without a lantern remains legal, if sometimes suspect. In civil actions the obligations of the harmed to furnish their own illumination figures in nuances of the prudence that keeps the honest from harm's way and raises now-awkward questions of carrying lanterns versus carrying handguns. The prudent carry a lantern or at least a bright cell phone screen. Rowboats abroad after nightfall must carry a clear-lens lantern or white flashlight, but the law obligates rowers to light them only when collision seems likely.

Fires, candles, lanterns, lighthouses, headlights, and screens emit light. The human eye turns toward emitted light (but away from the blinding sun) probably because humans are hard-wired to cherish fire. Aside from the sun, only the stars and lightning (and in swamps, will o' the wisp—momentarily ignited methane gas) emit light.[44] At night, amid reduced visual stimuli, the human eye fixes on firelight. Royal Marines training in the Arctic, holed up at night in gale-wracked tents, stare speechless at tiny gas stoves heating their dinners and breakfasts: they call the stoves "Commando Television."[45] Before gaslight (which rural dwellers understood as a quintessentially modern urban invention) and then electricity, and long before television and video monitors, firelight and candlelight drew the eye and held it. Indoors the flickering light cast all manner of shadows and, for those who stared into the flames or glowing embers, often induced a quasi-trancelike, hypnagogic state called **reverie**.[46] As stoves supplanted fireplaces and coal replaced wood, mid-nineteenth-century authors mused on changes in firelight, interesting themselves in the bluish glow of anthracite especially.[47] Outdoors, the pinpoint of firelight in otherwise encompassing darkness beckoned humans even as it deflected wolves, bears, catamounts, and other predators thought to shy from it. Firelight deflects demons and other supranatural beings too.

Fire means scent too, wafting in the dark, accentuating faint breezes and announcing the burning of oak or maple, hemlock or juniper. "The odor of burning juniper is the sweetest fragrance on the face of the earth, in my honest judgment: I doubt if all the smoking censers of Dante's paradise could equal it," mused Edward Abbey, a 1960s summer-only National Park Service ranger in remote Utah. He learned to leave his flashlight in his pocket because his eyes adapted to its small circle of light and ignored the vast surrounding dark, and to smell water from afar, or "at least, the smell of things associated with water—the unique and heartening odor of the cottonwood tree, for example, which in the canyonlands is the tree of life." His *Desert Solitaire: A Season in the Wilderness* emphasizes nighttime sensory acuteness, when stars glint "blue, emerald, gold," when Venus is the brightest object above, when it and starlight turn the cliffs "unnameable shades of violet," when the smoke from an unseen fire announces others bedding down for a cold night.[48] Twenty years before, he might have caught a whiff of coal smoke from a steam locomotive passing far off, one scent rural people knew not to chase. In his time, night trains existed chiefly as whistles in the dark.

The lost, the cold, the hungry struggled toward firelight, sometimes as unthinkingly as moths flutter into candles. Like mariners sailing toward harbors marked by lighthouses, travelers sought it, trudging toward beacons lit to guide them across foggy marshes and other bewildering places, and sometimes to betray them into peril.[49] Dampened fires and snuffed candles often left wayfarers as disoriented as false lights wrecked mariners. City-dweller apprehension of the dark, especially dark riven by driving rain or snow or great gales, bemuses rural people accustomed to night and raises disquieting fears of planetary power failure. The Carrington Event of 1859, a solar flare so massive it ignited the nascent telegraph networks of the United States and Great Britain, remains relatively unstudied but lately interests insurance companies and other long-term thinkers. A similar flare today would destroy all electronic and most electric devices instantly. Whatever the chances of a wayward meteor slamming into the earth, the possibilities of another great solar flare seem much higher. Night would return, urbane order perhaps collapse into mob rule and famine, and dark become terror, not the cozy, inveigling, embracing urban night Rolt remembered all his life, the night lit by the colors of candlelight, the flames of wood and coal fires, and the rare flaring of gaslight.

Any analysis of landscape proceeds by night as well as by day, and in all sorts of weather. In the clear air of the High Plains, nighttime long-distance views sometimes reveal a passenger train, its length brilliantly illuminated, moving like a line of ants in the far distance, then suddenly gone. After its passing, the observer knows that far off lies a railroad track but knows nothing of the color of the train itself.

Color shapes landscape, but few educated people know much about it, largely because even fewer see light acutely. From its inception in the 1840s, photography frustrated many would-be photographers, even long after George Eastman invented roll film and inexpensive box cameras. Otherwise smart, determined people failed to see light, and so they over- or underexposed film. Frustration drove the invention of actinometers by 1890, then photovoltaic meters, then cameras with meters coupled to shutter speed adjustments which made finicky color-film photography accessible to millions after the late 1940s. Monochrome photography, however wide its latitude for exposure miscalculation, nonetheless dismayed many would-be photographers: the sensitivity of color-negative and, especially, color-slide image making infuriated millions. Manufacturers of cameras, film, and processing materials found insensitivity to light well-nigh intractable. Their efforts to educate the public in composition largely succeeded, but over the whole of the twentieth century the firms failed to make the public understand that cameras and film record light (and sometimes color), not objects.

This is important. Eastman Kodak and other great firms funded extravagant educational operations. Free or low-cost magazines like *Kodakery*, brochures and technical leaflets distributed gratis in camera stores, and above all informational advertisements in photography magazines and a plethora of superb, low-priced informational booklets made photography an articulated extracurricular enterprise, not a schoolroom subject. From 1886 on, Eastman Kodak encouraged neophyte photographers to make images away from interruption. Only rarely did urban settings illustrate its counsels about film choice, composition, and—above all—lighting. The magazines urged readers to seek out places away from foot and vehicle traffic, away from side-walk jostling, away from rubberneckers and advice-givers, away from automobiles. It sent readers into rural places, knowing that in quiet spots photographers might work unhurried, might make the exposure-setting notes it advised, and might in time see the fall of light acutely and learn to record it using a multiplicity of lenses, films, and papers.[50]

Indirectly, Kodak and its competitors educated Americans in the moral picturesqueness of rural landscape. Neither in wilderness nor in cities did amateur photographers find the locations in which to sharpen their mastery of seeing light and—after the late 1930s invention of Kodachrome—color.

Indirectly too the camera companies alerted photographers (including professionals and serious amateurs) to the intermittent magic of photography. No matter how acutely photographers composed their would-be images and exposed their selected film, developed negatives now and then revealed things missed in the field.

Often photographers missed the fall of light. As Ursula K. Le Guin emphasizes in her 1968 *A Wizard of Earthsea*, magic can be the fall of light on a place. But the fall of light differs from place to place just as color does, and often climate governs the regularity of fall and color both. In 1937, just as manufacturers introduced color film, M. G. J. Minnaert published his seminal *Light and Color in the Outdoors*. Reprinted and revised over decades and still in print, it distinguishes a wealth of outdoor optical phenomena that educated people, even many painters, simply never realize. It also explains origins: gasoline and diesel engines "emit fine smoke which looks blue against a dark background. If, however, the smoke is seen against the light background of the sky, it does not appear to be blue at all, but yellow." Therefore, "the blueness is not an inherent property of the smoke in the way that the blue of blue glass is, but results from the smoke dispersing the blue rays more than the yellow or red ones," something especially noticeable in the exhaust of accelerating buses and in wood-fire smoke. Seen against dark conifers, the lower smoke from house chimneys is blue because observers see it through dispersed light, the upper smoke reddish because they see it through transmitted light. City buses once had street-level exhaust pipes, but new ones exhaust through roofs: despite pollution control devices, what Minnaert noted is still noticeable, just as columns of wood-stove smoke on calm days produce color striation, especially in mountain valleys. But localized fog, mist, and haze alone do not explain the bluish haze which invests the Smoky Mountains and other conifer-covered regions. Forests emanate terpenes and other organic vapors oxidized by sunlight and ozone into macromolecules which scatter light, and certain landforms contain the vapors in peculiar ways.[51]

An observer confronting foreground haze and background fog may realize that buildings appear extraordinarily high, but typically, Minnaert insists, "the combination of these impressions, which often is quite subconscious," gives a palatial stateliness to large buildings and other large objects. "Notice that *fog leaves the silhouettes of objects as sharp as they were.* Everything is covered in a veil of general light, so that contrasts become less marked, but there are no diffuse transitions from light to dark objects." Despite precise definition and explanation (and italics), Minnaert confronts the novel impact of color film on traditional aesthetics, including **stateliness** and other terms. "The splendid photographs of sunny mist in a wood are taken against the light with the camera pointing a little away from the sun," he explained of examples routinely shaping calendar illustration. But he knew too that most people looking at such mist or at photographs of it would not think about the lack of wind that enabled the mist to form and endure, however briefly. In long, windless periods, dust settles into the lowest levels of air, making visibility poor: "during windy, sunny weather," the rising air currents move dust particles upward, producing the usually unremarked better visibility of afternoon than of morning, of midsummer than of winter.[52] Smoke, dust, droplets, and along the beach salt crystals, all aerosols too rarely considered, transform light and landscape. So does smog.

Minnaert told photographers to stop making photographs and instead experiment with their colored filters, looking through a red filter when blue haze covers the distance to see things scarcely discernible in ordinary white light. He told everyone to walk in snow or along breakers on moonless nights, notice the brightness of whites, and wonder if the rods in the human eye are "especially sensitive to contrast at this low level of brightness." He directed attention at the regular variation in mowed-lawn rows, noting that rows appear much lighter when the direction of mowing is away from the viewer than when toward (when away, it reflects more light). He pointed out that a gravel road is "white-gray toward the sun, brown-gray away" and that in a wood on an autumn morning, in hazy air, the sun rays hit haphazardly but obviously among the trunks, their parallel lines bringing close "the fascination of aerial perspective."[53] So much of what people find delightful in scenery is rational, and understanding optics produces ever more acute observation and—perhaps—better photography and greater delight.

Like flight—especially in the local, small-scale ways Tomeï details—darkness, light, and photography prove too little studied in terms of individual landscape exploration. Digital image-making—including images made from amateur-flown drones—entrances users even if they pay little attention to cell phone and other lens optics, let alone to resolving power or the pixel-memory capturing of color.

Color rewards lifelong scrutiny. Its history proves rich, convoluted, and intricate, one juxtaposing Leonardo, Newton, and Goethe, variations in color terminology, discoveries in the physiology of the eye and the materiality of light, and individual differences in acuity and discrimination. "The sunshine dazzlingly accentuated the local colors, and even the shadowed portions were so luminous that they, relatively speaking, could have served as highlights. The same was true of the sea-green water. Everything was painted bright on bright," wrote Goethe of his first days in Italy in 1786. How children learn color and how color alters the emotions fascinated him. "We who live on ground that is either dirty and muddy or dusty, that is colorless and dims reflections, and who perhaps even live in narrow rooms, cannot independently develop such a cheerful eye," he determined of the Venetians.[54] How children learn includes childhood questions orbiting around orange as color and flavor against yellow and lemon, fireworks (gunpowder mixed with copper, antimony, and other metals to produce specific colors as emitted light), ocean-edge driftwood fires burning green and blue, and in the minds of children and homeowners, paint.

White paint, the first kind of paint produced in the newly independent United States, lives as the epitome of nationhood even if few remember why the taxpayers built a white house for their presidents. Color, its root words, the dull red of barns, the green of nineteenth-century passenger trains (why not brown?), the young black of newly asphalted roads, the enduring red of fire engines which goes to black at night in ways chartreuse does not, the rainbow of farm tractors (farm implement color often indicates quality of soil, green machinery costing more and appearing frequently on superb loam), and the amber of railroad and street signals and waves of grain deserve many books. Color shapes much of Donald D. Hoffman's incisive *Visual Intelligence: How We Create What We See*, a lucid, straightforward analysis of subtleties like the way a "photometer constructs the properties of light that it reports" and the fact that almost no one sees objects change color despite constant shifts in outdoor illumination as the sun moves and clouds intermittently obscure and reveal colors.[55] Hoffman reveals the biological (and learned) sources of compensation perceptions which make photographers so often dissatisfied with color film and which muddle the ways some inquirers record impressions and memories of landscape.

"Transferring experience from the vat of life into the vessel of the journal is a distillation: it sieves, concentrates, and ferments," writes Hannah Hinchman in *A Trail through Leaves: The Journal as a Path to Place*, a folio advancing her argument for a visual diary, a luminous sketchbook of event maps, pieces of landscape, and landscape happenings recorded in pencil drawings, watercolor, colored pencil, pen-and-ink vignettes, and quirky cameos. She argues for a journal unlike those of Thoreau and most travelers, a visual journal emphasizing light, form, and color expressed graphically, perhaps as art but certainly as a personal record. Magisterial and compelling, her book emphasizes how little children learn about drawing, the crudity and stupidity of early art education ("Now, most children have sets of big bright markers that don't blend very well, and they use them on absorbent newsprint or construction paper. No wonder they feel disappointed!"), the ways classroom color-inside-the-lines exercises stultify innate curiosity and blind children (and adults) to "a whole world of mixed, odd, changing, undefinable colors." In the Wyoming Badlands Hinchman gives order to what stunned Abbey: clear air, stark light, color beyond the boxed set, light and color demanding that the observer see acutely and mix colors precisely to realize the landscape, to make it real. In the abandoned mining camps and upland pastures and gulches, she finds that in an ever more visual society most adults share "the habit of seeing the world as dead," as still as a photographic "scene." Instead of realizing and experimenting with seeming optical (but really perceptual) illusions, most adults automatically ignore what they appear to see—say the way fireflies appear to fly upward each time they flash. Instead they see nature and landscape as fixed, still. They miss what she finds everywhere in Thoreau's journals, the ubiquitous flux most evident in light and color, and they miss too the opportunities implicit in "the act of recording a life, in healthy solitude and active connection to loved terrain."[56] Instead, most people stare at screens. Disciplined (and self-disciplined) to not see the vibrating color of the roadside, they do not explore, do not see, do not recall, do not get out of cars and walk and see and realize.

"I'd vote for solitary walking" over any sort of meditation therapy, she remarks courageously. "Stepping outside the comfortable padding of books, music, news, movies, magazines, conversations, all the reassuring attention-absorbers, is a necessary act of exposure." Exercise, especially walking, oxygenates the bloodstream and perhaps, she muses, "boosts the performance of the cone cells" in ways somehow analogous to the pupils contracting and expanding according to ambient light. In the end, Hinchman cares for effect, not physiological cause. "It's best to drop into a wander, with only a vague direction or perhaps a landmark to steer by."[57] Her book appeared in 1997, when many people, especially the young, already walked with earphones transmitting music. Now, when they walk with earbuds while staring at smart-phone screens, reading and texting and ignoring, its themes grow only more powerful and disconcerting.

Analyzing landscape empowers. Noticing—noticing without keeping any sort of journal, visual or otherwise—reveals and entices. Piecing together what one sees when one wanders or walks quickly on everyday errands requires only will and practice, not batteries and wireless connection. Journalizing helps almost certainly, but sustained scrutiny comes first. Scrutiny engenders wonder and energizes nascent curiosity. Exploring landscape, however casually, is a therapy and magic of its own.[58] But it depends on curiosity and scrutiny.

Formal education deprecates visual acuity. Herbert N. Casson asserts that "schools aim at pushing facts into children's memories," succeeding so well that by about age fourteen children ask fewer questions and notice less, or at least ask less about what they notice outside the classroom. His 1936 *The Priceless Art of Observation* emphasizes how few adults, especially in cities, devote much attention to their surroundings. Its arguments anticipate the 1970s findings of Stanley Milgram and other social scientists, who determined that city dwellers tune out almost all visual and spatial stimuli. For Casson, classroom emphasis on facts destroys abilities honed in the eras before mandatory schooling: students who survive formal education with curiosity and observational skills intact might find powerful positions if like adults encourage them. In manufacturing and retailing, for example, they bring "net-profit eyes" which identify bottlenecks or potential innovations, just as they improve the work of real estate agents by recognizing what most professionals ignore. But too few adults aid the rare teenagers who might become around age twenty the self-disciplined observers and explorers who find themselves well recompensed five years later—and happy and satisfied walking alone outdoors.[59]

Decades after Casson, well-educated adults now and then wonder about police officers, not only uniformed ones on patrol but plainclothes ones moving almost unidentified. What do the cops notice when they cruise down a suburban street? What do the rural deputy sheriff and Navajo Tribal Police officer realize as they look across miles of terrain that might entice Abbey and Hinchman and frighten most urban Americans? In the Old English word for spider, **attercop**, is the root of the modern English **cop**. Today cops throw out dragnets, but once medieval Englishmen knew sheriffs and reeves to spin **copwebs** (linguistic dyslexia changed the word to **cobweb**). Law-abiding, tax-paying, well-educated adults often fear the police even as they distrust them, but only rarely do they explore such feelings. Cops are observant and typically retentive and analytical concerning what they notice. Not well recompensed in salary but rewarded with thrills and satisfaction, they spend a lot of time just looking around and almost as much time remembering details of no immediate value in crime prevention and solution. Often they did badly in school. They looked out windows, seemed distracted in class, kept quiet about what they noticed while doing (or not doing) something required, all activities in which they delight today. Much of their work is preventive and much of that work involves conjuring landscape in multiple ways, often while thinking about different matters. One way to learn what cops and gazers notice is to browse Eric Partridge's *A Dictionary of the Underworld: British and American* and learn about panel-houses, shelfs (not shelves), drying rooms, and touch-offs.[60] And when a crime is reported, sergeants ask patrol officers what they noticed last week on Oak Street, and the sergeants (and victims and taxpayers) expect the cops to remember everything from the green, rusty van parked in a driveway to an unmown lawn to a coddled lap dog running free, covered in mud.

Cops notice other dedicated observers. Now and then they distrust them, especially if the observers carry large cameras (and perhaps tripods), but typically they recognize fellow analysts of nothing-in-particular, and watch. Sometimes they caution dedicated observers about wandering in high-crime areas or places otherwise dangerous, especially places abandoned by all but the homeless, felons, and addicts. And often they reveal themselves as deeply interested in all components of landscape, the light and color of places, the way natural systems work in specific locales (the stretch of road which freezes first, the storm drain system too small to carry off "gully-washer" rains, the path that leads from apartment complexes to the back parking lots of nearby malls, skirting swamps and marshes), the history of places and likely futures ("There was a railroad here, you know, and it might come back. See the line of light over there?"). As a group, cops might be the best-organized of all landscape observers, but organization itself is unnecessary.

Every individual creates landscape but not by shoveling earth, erecting buildings, felling forest. As Thoreau remarked, farmers might own the land, but the observant walker in time owns the landscape. Each inquirer creates a concatenation of space and structure peculiar to himself or herself simply by noticing. Frustration originates in analysis, in questioning, in hearing explanation accurately, in words and in the silences in which inquirers and the inquired-of grapple for words, for the right words. In the toolkit of landscape conjuring, words prove important.

A sandy way on a hot, bright American Southwest day curves deeper into the bosque, quasi-wild land nonetheless useful for grazing, especially by hardened longhorn cattle able to fend for themselves. JRS

2 CONSTRUCTS

Pronunciation conceals and reveals. **Moth** boasts two pronunciations lexicographers assert correct: the plural **môthz** suggests one is more powerful and—perhaps—more correct. However lexicographers dispute the roots of **moth**, they appear resigned to the word concealing two different roots so far untraceable in writing and in print. Choosing one variant or the other reveals speaker traits, especially class and nationality, perhaps otherwise masked. Writers and readers tend to dismiss issues of pronunciation. The tendency proves unwise.

"'Spreet' and 'wangs' should be spelt 'sprit' and 'vangs,'" asserted one frustrated British yachtsman in 1971. "However I think it is easier to write what is said, rather than worry about the correct spelling. Wangs are always wangs; spreet alters only in the word sprits'l."[1] The yachtsman, D. H. Clarke, owned a near-derelict Thames sailing barge, an eighty-foot cargo vessel built along lines derived three centuries earlier from Dutch prototypes. Rigged in a peculiar, enduring form whose parts retained their seventeenth-century Dutch names, the last of the barges freighted the correct pronunciation of words long spelled differently than spoken. Wooden-boat enthusiasts encourage boatbuilders and commercial fishermen to write books about their crafts. Often written by authors lacking any editorial help, sometimes printed rather than published, such books unwittingly emphasize ordinary use of words obsolescent except alongshore. Their ostensible subjects notwithstanding, they prove a superb introduction to issues of landscape terminology, including pronunciation clues to old meanings.

A school dropout who started fishing aboard venerable luggers in 1964 at age sixteen, Paul Greenwood recalls in *Once Aboard a Cornish Lugger* words and phrases then long obsolete on land—**scruffer, scruffing, tachins, maund baskets**, and "raising a scry," among others—all of which he brusquely defines. But utterly unselfconsciously he uses **bedtide, scunned**, and other words as though readers know them as ordinary mainstream 2007 British English.[2] He and Clarke confront brute necessity. Wooden-boat aficionados see a part of sailing-vessel rigging or something about an old-fashioned net being buoyed and ask, "What is that part called?" Often what they get is everyday working English alien to lexicographers and other landsmen, the sort of surprise that hit Clarke, exhausted after a storm, his barge leaking, when he managed to put into Happisburgh. He learned locals pronounced the name "Haisbra."

Landsmen reading his book may pause at the phrase "ruck the tops'l" and even after searching good dictionaries know little.[3] **Rucking** a triangular sail means lowering its peak without reefing its foot. **Rucking** and **reefing** are maritime cousins of topographical terms. Ruck terrain challenges hikers shouldering rucksacks. Reefs challenge anyone inquiring into essential landscape. Some never submerged at high tide sport crude navigational aids. Do the aids alone transform wilderness into shaped land, into landscape?

Language offers hints. Words stick to the ground. Modern English is deeply rooted in Celtic, Old English, and Old Frisian, with strong overlays of Old Norse and Norman French. Rising sea levels once overwhelmed terrestrial wilderness and bits of landscape. The shallow, stormy North Sea (named by Frisians looking north) covers land once connecting present-day England with what is now the Netherlands. Old English and Old Frisian prove eerily similar. Speakers of modern English, especially those raised along the east coast of England, find they know Old Frisian words but less often modern Dutch ones. Frisian, or Fris, remains a flourishing minority language in Europe, used by about 800,000 people in the Netherlands and northwestern Germany. Old Norse fuels the enduring Scandinavian bias of coastal people troubled by Viking raids and forever changed by Norse settlement between 800 and 1066. Norman French, what jurists still call **law French**, arrived with the Norman Conquest, whispers still in the British Channel Islands, and echoes in legal records, especially old deeds, sometimes confounding attorneys and landowners across the United States. One finds much of it picked apart in Randle Cotgrave's 1611 *Dictionarie of the French and English Tongues* and the five-volume *Dictionnaire universel françois et latin* of 1732. A good place to start in the fourth

volume is under **pays**. How **landscape** and **countryside**
relate deserves a long book indeed.[4] How "landscape" translates into languages other than English must perplex any
English-speaking traveler learning and using any other language. But "pays" is nowhere near a synonym of "landscape."[5] That is not a quibble. It is something important
and inconvenient to contemporary translators of English
and French thinking about the dry surface of the earth and
afraid of swimming in surf.

Superb modern dictionaries, especially the *Oxford English Dictionary*, trace root words and usage over time, but
others sometimes do better, even old etymologies like Walter
W. Skeat's 1881 *Etymological Dictionary of the English Language*, Joseph T. Shipley's 1945 *Dictionary of Word Origins*,
and Eric Partridge's 1959 *Origins: A Short Etymological Dictionary of Modern English*.[6] Abel Boyer's *Royal Dictionary* of
1699 (repeatedly revised long after his death, including "sea
terms and sea phrases" added in 1819), Samuel Johnson's
1755 *Dictionary of the English Language* (frequently revised),
William Falconer's 1769 *Universal Dictionary of the Marine*
(often updated), James Orchard Halliwell's idiosyncratic
Dictionary of Archaic and Provincial Words (1847), and
Richard Stephen Charnock's 1859 *Local Etymology: A
Derivative Dictionary of Geographical Names* open on mysteries, local usage, and intractable problems of translation
that Jürgen Schäfer grapples with in his 1989 *Early Modern
English Lexicography* and Laura Wright dredges up in her
1996 *Sources of London English: Medieval Thames Vocabulary*. Francis Grose's 1785 *Classical Dictionary of the Vulgar
Tongue* opens on the earthy, while John Russell Bartlett's

1848 *Dictionary of Americanisms: A Glossary of Words and Phrases Usually Regarded as Peculiar to the United States* presages the modern *Dictionary of American Regional English.* No dictionary is perfect. None is the para-authority of spoken and written English.

The *OED*, so often regarded as the arbiter, the final word in historical and contemporary usage, often ignores nuances vital in any determined inquiry into landscape, especially alongshore and in agricultural areas. The 1914 *Century Dictionary: An Encyclopedic Lexicon of the English Language* makes that clear in its twelve volumes. As Boyer knew firsthand, translating landscape words from English into French proves maddening, words from elsewhere sometimes even more so, and words used by coastal mariners vexing beyond measure. *OED* lexicographers still cannot place **culvert** in context. The word appeared from nowhere around 1770, not from Latin or French (no connection with **covert** seems likely), perhaps from some dialect English spoken by canal laborers. As the designation for a tunneled drain, it materialized fully formed in late eighteenth-century engineering documents. The *Century* editors struggled to know how an African-Bahamas word denoting salt water inland from a barrier beach (often studded with mangroves) might apply a hundred miles west on the Georgia coast (see under **swash** and **swashbuckler**). Only six years later, A. Ansted, a specialist lexicographer, noted in *A Dictionary of Sea Terms* that **swash** denoted a shoal in a tideway, usually found at the mouth of an estuary, and **swashway** named a channel cut through estuarine shoals by "a peculiar set of the tide, which also keeps it from silting in." Ansted knew the term only as one regularly used on the east coast of Britain. He knew too that mariners and well-educated yachtsmen sailing out of London pronounced it "swatch."[7] Scholars deeply interested in landscape and architectural terminology now and then discover all manner of variant meanings. In sixteenth-century Italy, for example, some Venetian words named exactly the opposite of what they designated in Florence.[8] In Lowestoft, a harbor town on the east coast of England, people call steeply staired alleys running down to the sea **scores**: their everyday use of the ancient term (rooted in the Old English **scor**, designating twenty, shown as a long notch made on a reckoning stick) seems to have escaped most lexicographers and urban designers.[9] Any inquiry into landscape vocabulary immediately produces entrancing and puzzling questions about the meanings of words long ago written down as pronounced by educated people unaware of complex denotations and connotations.

But lexicographical complexity scarcely hinders contemporary theorists from embracing some dictionary definitions of **landscape** over others. To many theorists, the *OED* reigns as the para-authority, the unquestionable (and unquestioned) revered standard. Indeed, this is exactly what its publishers desire: the *OED* originated in the heyday of British imperialism and endures as one of the stunning powers of empire building. Nineteenth-century imperialist mistranslations of "landscape" skewed how a few late 1930s American scholars determined the word might designate part of the academic discipline of geography.[10] What they supposed were the German roots of "landscape" produced tensions remarkably like those swirling around contemporary efforts to replace

landscape (in British and American geographical theory) with **pays**.[11] German geographers and British translators of the 1880s missed what J. ten Doornkaat Koolman implies in his 1882 *Wörterbuch der ostfriesischen Sprache* and Jan de Vries and F. de Tollenaere note in their *Nederlands etymologisch woordenboek*, the expression **uitgestrektheid land,** designating land overlooked from some elevation, however slight, which entered English circa 1598 and then fused with another imported term.[12] The German experts missed (perhaps deliberately) the Old Frisian and West Frisian roots of the modern Dutch term **landschap**. Despite the efforts of Frisian and Dutch lexicographers, few English writers look beyond the *OED*, a dictionary which still reflects bias against dialect-based, spoken, working-class terminology in favor of what literary-minded, middle-class Victorians prized.[13] Its editors have never been very much interested in culverts, let alone those who made them or crawled through them. Almost never do inquirers into **landscape** examine the word in the 1988 *Chambers Dictionary of Etymology*. Navigating swatches in linguistic arguments tests anyone, especially anyone remotely familiar with the limitations of translation and unabridged dictionaries or anyone who has ever gotten lost in the rural areas of any country other than his own.

Hinchman argues that learning to draw and to paint as a child makes an adult resilient in the visual tsunami of contemporary mass-media, electronic-based living. Knowing about landscape terms, actively considering them, toughens the walker in rucked space. Today global-minded walkers find the stubborn staying power of regional and local usage

everywhere away from cities—and occasionally in the pur-
lieus of cities too. Sometimes they trip over it, as do careful
readers of land conveyances, travel accounts, and crime
novels, sources the *OED* still slights.

Roaming in dictionaries and other reference works,
including old editions of encyclopedias, gazetteers, and *Roget's
Thesaurus* (not the thesauri slyly dovetailed into word-pro-
cessing software), proves one way to explore landscape.[14]
Collecting old dictionaries and other reference works tends
to be inexpensive. A small but useful library costs less than
the high-tech gear worn by explorers in rain, deep cold, and
gales. Inquiring into many local or idiosyncratic works, one
discovers how often they began in direct experience. Halliwell's two-volume dictionary originated in his careful walking, listening to locals, and above all scrutinizing what he
saw. His 1861 *Rambles in Western Cornwall* recounts his
diverging from paths and roads and cutting across fields and
through hedges, what he calls **scrambling**, in search of things
only elderly country people could name—and in search of
old-timers who could name the things onto which he stum-
bled.[15] Among other alongshore ephemeral phenomena they
named **acker**, "a kind of eddying twirl when the river is
flooded, which is often extremely dangerous to bargemen."[16]
What they named they knew as important, even deadly, even
if only locally.[17] It thrived beyond the ken of most lexicographers, at the marges of "landscape" and landscape.

Old littoral landscape terminology is rarely abscondite.
It survives (and sometimes flourishes) *in place* in the
Norman Archipelago, Guernsey, Jersey, and the other
Channel Islands, all long part of the United Kingdom but

speaking neither English nor French but a tongue grounded in ancient Norman and salted with Old Norse and Old Frisian. The oft-derided (in Britain and France), obsolescent dialect rewards linguists, who find it rich in roots and survivals and mystery. The ending **-ey** as in **Guernsey**, **Jersey**, and **Alderney** is the Old Norse word for **island**, and the Frisian term **gers**, meaning **grassy**, may have amalgamated with it to produce **Guernsey**, a grassy island.[18] Pronunciation and grammar, especially nasal consonants, distinguish the core of the dialect, but Guernésiais and its cousins share a unique and resilient vocabulary. Scholars tend to identify its regular speakers with what one calls "low socioeconomic status" and residence outside the few towns on the islands, and emphasize that each island boasts multiple subtly variant subdialects.[19] But the speakers comprehend a language rich in terms for plants, birds, and other objects of great interests to coastal fishermen and farmers, one rooted in Latin and in a series of linguistic near-conquests.[20]

In the Bay of St. Malo just off the coast of Normandy any patient traveler can learn words evolved from Latin and shaped by Old Norse, Old Frisian, and several distinct epochs of French and English. **Couture** identifies fields reclaimed from the sea, **caoste** means coast, **bequet** an extremity of land, **mielles** and **dicqs** dunes, **friquet** waste land (in British English, a small lea), **preel** a small meadow, **bigard** a triangular enclosure of land, **vazon** a salt marsh, **nocq** a narrow conduit to the sea. Islanders have specific terms for fairies (**pouques** and **fâes**) and goblins (**haptalons**), glimmerings of light (**beluettes**), and spider crabs (**houvlin**), just as they have for a long crest of land (**gron**) and a small peninsula (**houmet**). Much of the landscape vocabulary emphasizes stones and stonework. **Énne mescelle**, designating stone field-gate posts, especially fixes lexicographer attention, since the posts seem more likely to be prehistoric standing stones, for which the islanders have two words (one probably derived from Old Norse), **bourg** and **pouquelae**. Much of archipelago language is altumal, including a whole set of terms for the rigging of sailing ships and another for types of waves which hit the islands.[21] In the fifteen years he lived in the archipelago as a political exile after 1855, the novelist Victor Hugo did more than write *Les Misérables* and other novels: he studied the dialects. He set his *Toilers of the Sea* in the islands and made one dialect word so famous that it replaced its modern French counterpart. He used **pieuvre**, the insular term for devilfish or octopus, instead of **poulpe**. In a gripping chapter describing an island man snatched by an octopus, Hugo elevated one archipelago term to an enduring place in standard French.

Until late in the twentieth century no accurate English translation of the novel existed. The first translators bowdlerized the text. "Gone were the underwater pebbles resembling the heads of green-haired babies, the evocation of springtime as the wet dream of the universe, and, of course, the nightmarish anatomy of the *pieuvre* with its single orifice," writes Graham Robb in his introduction to James Hogarth's modern, complete translation. Hugo loved "the craggy consonants of English," but he misunderstood pronunciation, using "bug-pip" for "bagpipe" and "dik" for "dike," among other errors at which British critics guffawed. But until recently, English translators omitted an entire chapter, "The Sea and the Wind," about the great storms which sweep the islands, and butchered lines like "a breakwater is a combination of what is known in France as a groyne and in England as a dike."[22] Hugo misunderstood the pronunciation of "dike," but he knew dikes keep out water: his translators substituted "dam," an embankment that keeps water in.

Translators mangled an early chapter, "The Old Language of the Sea," in which Hugo demonstrated not only the richness of archipelago seafaring terms and the difficulties posed by their pronunciation, but the force with which they clashed with post-1820 French. "A specialist archaeologist could have gone there to study the ancient language, used in working ships," he concluded of terms varying from one island to another and revealing much about deep origins. But even **patarasse**, a caulker's iron, Hogarth mistranslates as a "caulker's chisel."[23] And the Jersey **cannel**, designating a **gutter**—a narrow ditch wider than a **grindle** or **vennel** but narrower than a **gut** dug through saltmarsh—endures as a Norman-Latin term designating a built form almost unknown inland of New England saltmarshes, a ditch most unlike urban gutters but well known to swamp-Yankee estuary adventurers.[24]

Channel Islands speech offers a splendid portal on landscape and language, and Hugo's long-mistranslated novel warns contemporary readers that translators often misunderstand elusive dialect or terms from obsolescent languages, especially those used precisely by polyglot mariners. "People may be better acquainted with *Heart of Darkness* than with *Nostromo* only because the former is exceedingly short, as

well as amenable to skimming, on account of a thin plot and
lengthy landscape descriptions," warns intelligence analyst
Robert L. Kaplan in *The Coming Anarchy: Shattering the
Dreams of the Post Cold War*. "In *Nostromo*, however, landscape ambience is a tightly controlled, strategic accompani-
ment to political realism."[25] Joseph Conrad understood the
vagaries of landscape and language in the limicole realm,
where sea and land meet and coastal people meet strangers
continuously. Kaplan asserts that "it is a tribute to Conrad's
insight that his description of Costaguana and its port,
Sulaco, captures so many of the crucial tidbits and subtleties
about troubled Third World states (particularly small and
isolated ones) that foreign correspondents of today experience but do not always inform their readers about."[26] Landscape acquires peculiar importance in archipelagos and other
limicole places because it reflects the ebb and flow of seaborne force which often leaves **ackers** in its wake.

As C. S. Nicholls notes in *The Swahili Coast*, **swahili**
designates in Arabic anything "belonging to the coast." He
details how Omani traders around 1802 began using the
term to designate people "who inhabited the East African
coast from the mouth of the River Juba in the north to Cape
Delgado in the south."[27] Although it was recorded once in
1331 by Ibn Battuta, a wide-ranging traveler exploring the
coast of what is present-day Tanzania, the Portuguese who
colonized the region beginning in the fifteenth century
never recorded the term: Omanis perhaps knew Ibn Battuta's *Voyages* when they colonized Zanzibar. Britons perhaps
took the word from them.[28] Along the coast of Colombia
today locals speak dialects grounded in sixteenth-century

Andalusian. Seville and Cadiz produced most of the mariners who settled that coast and who kept it connected with Spain even after independence. In his *Léxico hispanoamericano del siglo XVI*, Peter M. Boyd-Bowman traces not only pronunciation but the meanings of words long obsolescent except in specific places in what was formerly New Spain. His *From Latin to Romance in Sound Charts* details change powerful among elites (especially urban elites) but scarcely noticed in the Channel Islands and elsewhere: his work on the regional origins of early New Spain colonists illuminates enduring site-specific dialect.[29] The Colombian coast (as Conrad knew in sailing-ship days) is poor, and most of it remains as unvisited as much of the Tanzanian coast. Isolation preserves ancient terms and often produces new ones despite the power of radio and even television.

Today in the mountains of northern New Mexico, most of the seemingly Spanish irrigation terms prove Arabic: they merged into Spanish during the Moorish occupation of the southern Iberian peninsula, especially around Seville. Navajo mechanics use well more than a hundred modern Navajo terms to identify automobile parts and repair processes: they easily and confidently eschew English terms.[30] Isolation matters, even near cities.

Massachusetts South Shore and Cape Cod people still use words (like **guzzle**, a low spot on a barrier beach over which pass neap tides and hurricane-driven surf) as people do on the Maine coast, which South Shore people settled in the late seventeenth century: pronunciation and vocabulary differ around Boston Harbor, on Cape Ann, and the New Hampshire coast.[31] As Raoul de la Grasserie points out in his 1909 *Des parlers des différentes classes sociales*, grammar, pronunciation, and vocabulary vary by class, and upper-class people tend to avoid rural areas, including the seacoast before the resort era. They and educated professional people often know only mainstream language and lack any awareness of, let alone knowledge of, local landscape terms including pronunciation, connotation, and folkloric significance. Second-generation educated people often scorn what they deem lower-class terminology: they fear using it will betray their humble origins.[32] However arty today, "the bosom of the deep" connotes placid mid-ocean swells. But the phrase can still mean sheltered inlets, the Lagoon of Venice, the inlets of Cape Cod, when they are not **holes**, as in Woods Hole, a harbor whose name puzzles rare tourists from Jackson Hole in Wyoming who dislike learning that in times of stress mariners like to put in to safety, between the breasts of the land.[33]

Global travel now often takes the form of urban or beach tourism, the latter sometimes involving ecotourism. In Cadiz, once the port of entry connecting Spain with its empire, and upstream in Seville, the inquirer discovers a rare mix of architecture and language. Until early in the twentieth century the Guadalquivir offered oceangoing sailing ships access to Cadiz. Tourists in Seville may admire the converted mosques and other structures built by Arabs who vanished late in the fifteenth century, but they may also hear pronunciation and vocabulary they encounter in the southern Caribbean. In the Baltic (or anywhere aboard Swedish steamships), they may admire bioluminescence on still, moonless nights, but only if they ask the Swedish term do they hear the word **mareld** and—perhaps—begin to wonder at the Nordic root words **mar** and **eld**, which produce the English **nightmare** and **eldritch**.[34] On the coast of Tuscany they may learn the word **maremma**, a word designating low-lying saltmarshes once thought pestilential in summer. Though coastal people use old words among themselves, often the terms slip into standardized language visitors use for something new to them. But often locals fear being thought uneducated, too poor to know radio and television, or benighted, and so struggle to use standard vocabulary.

Mountain people act similarly. Tourists (and tourism development officials) often prize or dismiss them as isolated and quaint, but learning topographical vocabulary alerts thoughtful travelers to occluded importances. At the southern end of the Sawatch, the Rocky Mountains split into the San Juan range to the west and the Sangre de Cristo in the east: the seasonally well-watered San Luis Valley, part of the Rio Grande headwaters, includes the spectacular gorge north of Taos. Tourists photograph the silver thread far below from marked photo-op spots but scarcely glance at the quasi-arid terrain sprinkled with chamisa and small cactus. To the locals, the whole region, including the better-watered river bottoms and arroyos punctuated with willow, cottonwood, and Russian olive, is **bosque**, a term novelist B. J. Oliphant uses precisely in her mysteries.[35] "Bosque" is mainstream Spanish for the mainstream American-English **forest**, the Spanish of Castile (not Seville) translating into the newspeak of American network television as **forest** or **woods**. In the San Luis Valley, inquiring travelers driving rutted dirt roads must listen with courtesy, sometimes at length, to hear locals use "bosque" otherwise. If they know the sumptuous English word **bosk**, they will hear coastal colonial Spanish echoing along rivers flooding after snow-melt and often drying at midsummer. "Bosk" denotes scrubby woods or clusters of thickets in larger glades, what utility line crews, ranchers, and railroaders call **brush**.

In his 1859 *Dictionary of Americanisms* John Russell Bartlett understood "brush" as a contraction of the English **brushwood** and emphasized that it included the branches of mature trees.[36] Asking tourists (especially urban tourists) "what all that is" while gesturing at the terrain reaching end-lessly away from the photo-op areas produces headshakes, shudders, and **no-man's land**, the last grounded in World War I trench warfare military jargon. Never do tourists use "bush," a powerful Australian term and once strong every-where east of the Mississippi. "The word 'bush' has retained in America the original meaning of the Dutch *bosch* more faithfully than in England, where it generally designates a single shrub, while here ... it means rather a region abound-ing in trees and shrubs," wrote Shele de Vere in his 1872 *Americanisms*.[37] Forty years later in her *New Dictionary of Americanisms*, Sylva Clapin emphasized that the term denoted "land covered with rank shrubbery. The primeval or virgin forest land. A thicket of trees. Uncultivated land covered with trees and undergrowth"—a definition empha-sizing regional diversity.[38] In the mountains of New Hamp-shire and Vermont the term flourishes in **sugar bush** and **maple bush**, but elsewhere Americans who still speak of being **bushed** or **bushwhacking** (especially when seeking out boundary lines or hunting) avoid using "bush," perhaps because the great prairies pioneers encountered after leaving the Appalachians forests (in Michigan, where dense forest morphed into discrete woods punctuating prairies, terrain pioneers named **openings** in ways that shaped James Fenimore Cooper's 1848 novel *The Bee-hunter; or, The Oak Openings*) predisposed even New Yorkers to abandon a word rooted in Dutch, used everywhere along the Atlantic coast, and met in slightly different form west of the Rio Grande.[39] Only in the northern Great Lakes states (and in Canada) do loggers use "bush" as Australians use it, to define any sort of back country with or without tall trees.[40]

South along the Rockies came the French *coureurs du bois* (the dry land beyond the Missouri basin deflected the voyageurs and their canoes), trapping and hunting their way until they met the northernmost outposts of New Spain, where many settled. In the San Luis Valley some of the oldest families have French surnames, but the word **bosque** flourishes, not **bois** and not **bush**, not even **brushland**, and not **scrub**, even though Washington Irving, in his 1832 *Tour of the Prairies*, remarked on "a toilsome and harassing march of two hours over ridges of hills covered with a ragged, meagre forest of scrub-oaks, and broken by deep gullies."[41] Today a tourist hiking into the bosque might take a backpack or knapsack, the latter known too by the word **rucksack**, rooted in the old English term **ruck**, for wrinkle, the ridge-and-valley appearance Irving noted. In rising wind some yachtsmen still "scandalize the mainsail," lowering its peak but not reefing its foot: working seamen ruck the sail, using the old word for wrinkle that names a shapeless sack rarely stuffed full.[42] In the Southwest, "bosque" now connotes not only a sort of vegetation but a sort of terrain, rucked terrain.

Across Acadian Canada (Quebec and wherever to the east some French-ancestry families remain following the last of what rural New Englanders call "the Old French Wars") survive some of the eight hundred words and many idioms invented by the mid-sixteenth-century writer François Rabelais.[43] Newfoundland outport villagers use **room** to designate the larger plot of land owned by an extended family and accessible to any family member choosing to build a house.[44] All the traveler, hiker, or canoeist must do is listen. Reading is good, but listening often reveals much more. Hinchman hits it right: walking alone proves a sort of meditation, and being alone encourages a brief conversation with someone encountered in place, someone who knows the words.

Too few inquirers into landscape learn much from seemingly uneducated people, children included, largely because most inquirers are well schooled but frequently ignorant not just of vocabulary but of light, color, atmospheric conditions, and other constituents of landscape vital to locals. "Modern 'literate' man often forgets that those who have never learned how to read and write possess far more retentive memories than the literate," asserts Ernle Bradford in *Mediterranean: Portrait of a Sea*. Memory often functions orally, wholly with spoken and heard words in ways reminding university-educated people of half-heard lectures on *The Odyssey* or *The Iliad* or perhaps *Beowulf.* "The visual memory is more highly developed in men who have never had to tax their brains with the printed word, and the senses are also equally sharpened in those who live a simple life close to the elements," Bradford observes.[45]

Bradford spent most of his life in the Mediterranean, sailing a small boat, visiting Levanzo and other out-of-the-way islands at length, basing his endeavors in Malta, noting not only the roots of thousands of dialect words but at least some ways in which illiterate locals understood landscape created over millennia. Attentive to light and color, the sky, irrigation ditches, and goat paths, as well as military, ecclesiastical, and civil building, Bradford found fishermen, peasant farmers, and other people embracing and easily using knowledge lost to their "educated" contemporaries. While perhaps not as sophisticated as that of English poet and essayist Robert Graves who made his life in Majorca,[46] Bradford's understanding of isolated-area vocabulary sometimes runs deeper. He knew of Sicilian fishermen tasting the wind, Maltese peasant farmers making accurate three-month weather forecasts, and innumerable comments about built form by the descendants of the builders dead a thousand years. Unlike Graves, Bradford had no classical education. He discovered the Mediterranean as a Royal Navy seaman in World War II, loved it on first sight, returned in a small sailing boat, and never left. More than most travelers, he had time to get to know the locals well enough to learn something of what they knew. He had no inhibitions about learning from the poor and the poorly educated.

Travelers, tourists, visitors (**visit** derives from the same root as **visual** and properly denotes seeing, not having a chat), embedded journalists and scholars, garrison troops, even castaways often learn little of what locals know. Sometimes questions embarrass locals, who keep silent, but more often than not, general questions produce only general, media-shaped answers, given in standard words locals assume newcomers know. Specific questions, ones about the name of a farm implement for example, frequently produce the common-based response, not a local-usage one revealing greater riches of origins and usages. Only when an inquirer from afar asks sideways do questions elicit what unlettered locals know.

Alphabetical dictionaries (and most are, including translation ones) sometimes do less well than topical ones, what lexicographers designate onomasiological ones. Thesauri are the best-known topical lexicons, grouping synonyms and near-synonyms according to some larger frame. Peter Mark Roget's 1852 *Thesaurus of English Words and Phrases* directs the reader to clusters of words as seventeenth-century (and earlier) dictionaries did: in it **channel** appears in a cluster of terms designating passages of water, among them **sough**, **gully-hole**, **race**, and **gutter**.[47] Topical dictionaries, especially dialect-based ones, are rare indeed, but imagining words as parts of larger clusters alerts the landscape inquirer, especially in foreign places, especially among farmers, fishermen, and other people working closely with land and sea, that one out-of-the-ordinary word often has kissing cousins worth learning. Until about 1800 many travelers carried topical translation dictionaries, not alphabetical ones, in part because they often spoke with uneducated people.[48]

No dictionary records every meaning of each headword. A traveler listening acutely and sometimes prompting gently may discover nuances which illuminate landscape and language alike.[49]

All alongshore, especially in northwest France, the Low Countries, the northwest corner of Germany, but even more in the British Isles and the Atlantic coast of North America, the careful inquirer, one who scrutinizes, asks obliquely, and hears intently, learns words beyond **gutter.** The word **gut**, designating a small, typically narrow channel, is related to **gatt**, a broad opening in an estuary: Hull Gut in Massachusetts Bay is narrow, deep, and dangerous; Fishermen's Gatt in the Thames Estuary is broad and easy sailing. Both take their names from Old Frisian and Old Dutch words.[50] In salt marshes and other low-lying areas drained through sluices at low tide, the walker hears **gate** and **gateway** often. Lexicographers know little of what the *Oxford English Dictionary* calls the "ulterior etymology" of **gate**. The word is old, **geat** in Old English and corresponding perfectly to the Old Frisian **gat** and **jet**, meaning "a hole or opening," the Old Frisian (and Old Norse) term enduring in the Dutch **gat**. But its pronunciation varied by region in what is now England, and in Northumberland and north Devon survives as **get** (although the word itself is not derived from the roots of the modern **get**) and in Kent as **gat**. The more connected an English place was (and maybe is) to Frisia (and, in time, the Netherlands), the more likely it is that locals pronounce the term differently than mainstream English speakers. But then again, the locals know a **gate** or **gateway** as a purpose-built opening in a dike through which water jets at ebb and flood tide, an opening perhaps controlled by boards, one connecting gutters and sea. The Old Frisian connection is strong, as it is in "gutter." English speakers rarely know the North Frisian, the now-German term **siel**. And everyone knows that without maintenance, gates betray in great storms, admitting the sea, eroding into uselessness, or jamming with the debris that ends all hope of drainage. Even in remote, seemingly unpeopled coastal areas, places where farming on reclaimed land has failed, most gates exhibit care.

But in Scandinavia, where **gata** in Norway and Sweden (and **gade** in Denmark) designates a narrow street or alley, what **gasse** identifies in German, flourishes a word which briefly influenced English. In Spenser's time, to the northeast of London, **gate** named also a street, a usage which disappeared, became a ruin, collapsed into **runagate**.[51] Running is one thing, running agate is running without reason, and "runagate" is a word useful in annoying urban designers, even renegade ones. Sometimes gates guard alleys from the runagate and sometimes "runagate" connotes an amazing, mazy alley, like Diagon Alley (perhaps named after a respected British manufacturer of binoculars?) in J. K. Rowling's *Harry Potter* books. Gates usually have keepers, lax and otherwise.

Alongshore the walker finds few ruined gates. Locals cajoled into talking about them know that where the sea has been it may well return, that making landscape is one thing, keeping it another—keeping out the sea strains human will and strains language too.

Asking about ruins makes locals pause. Remarking on recent ruins stops talk, even makes some locals turn away. Ruins other than preserved ruins with admission booths and guides and restrooms, with tour buses idling downhill, vex locals, force them to think of the past, of failure.[52] Ruins litter most landscapes. Like reefs and ledges they wreck adventures into knowing. Bradford knew this well, in his heart. Ruins five hundred years old, in open view of farmers and fishermen, stopped conversation before it started. Alongshore, ruins often whisper of other people, strangers, foreigners, and trouble from over the horizon. "The coast is clear" means one thing to smugglers, something else to people forever watchful for invaders, especially those who come in the dark or in fog.

In 1960 archaeologists Helge and Anne Ingstad, having worked their way north from Rhode Island attempting to match harbors and other coastal features with those mentioned in Norse sagas of lands beyond present-day Greenland, arrived at Cape Bauld in the north of Newfoundland aboard a tiny hospital ship making its rounds of remote villages.[53] As usual, they asked locals about the slightest indications of old mounds or long-forgotten building. A commercial fisherman, George Decker, suggested they go to Black Duck Brook by an open area he called "Lancy Meadow." They found and subsequently excavated the first known Norse settlement in North America, where today tourists visit the historic site at L'Anse-aux-Meadows. The Ingstads had luck on their side. Decker, known locally for his observational skills and thoughtfulness, had noticed the faintest of lines in the growth of grass, not mounds or foundations, and thought them worth mentioning. His local pronunciation endures despite formal topographical orthography.[54]

Any newcomer, especially any transient, must work hard to notice and understand what locals understand as derelict, abandoned, ruinous, pieces of landscape not ordinarily mentioned aloud and then often in ruined words.[55] South of Newfoundland, on the Maine coast, visitors find stone walls and cellar holes in the wind-bruised woods and other indications of withdrawal, if not absolute failure. Gerald Warner Brace, a long-time summer visitor deeply curious about what he saw and willing to patiently question locals often unwilling to speak easily, concluded that "man's grasp is not anywhere near as good as his reach." Climate, weather, poor soil, economic downturns, and other challenges defeated human nature and strength. Among the tiny, well-kept saltwater farms which delighted tourists lay hidden the ruins of countless long-afforested others. Each existing farm "took a stout body and soul to keep it all going from light to dark every day for a lifetime," Brace mused in *Between Wind and Water* six years after the Ingstad discovery. What could an inquirer know of how the farmer and his wife thought about the effort? Brace imagined that the farmer "probably reckoned his tasks something like this: roof to re-shingle, gutters rotten, paint in poor shape, pasture fence about gone, alders crowding in, blade on mower busted, wheel off the rake, horse seems to have colic, off ox is lame, hay still wet—needs turning—pond dry, dam broken some-where, weeds in the beans, corn pretty pindling, rust in the pump water—or is it mud?" Brace avoided how the farmwife might have thought of what was around her: two generations earlier, Sarah Orne Jewett in *The Country of the Pointed Firs* and other books had faced that, as Ruth Moore did a genera-tion later. In a cold, harsh, thin-soil place, Brace concluded, "the gospel of work is a fine one in a world of strong and capable people, but when work is too much and bodies too weak, desperation can result. Or simply defeat, or resigna-tion, or the imperceptible sinking and letting go."[56]

His books number among the starkest of any focused on the abandonment so obvious to any walker in northern New England and further north after about 1850. Brace noted: "The farm places could crumble away in rot and litter, and many did, even in the good old days. Perhaps it was the women who held them together, those strong characters recorded so often in literature, dedicated wholly to cleanliness and godliness." In the end, what Brace concludes of northern New England seems true of vast reaches of cold land, especially when trapping, hunting, and fishing give out, when no oil or mineral keeps money moving: "Life in the northeastern coast has been thought to be too wintry and hard for the best kind of culture. All efforts go into survival in the year-round war with cold weather."[57] No matter how polite, the summer visitor remarking on ruins directs the attention of locals to what may well befall their own enterprises. In the autumn, or even in summer when heavy clouds break the sun, they know those enterprises as **pindling**, an old New England term, a woman's word, a word itself a ruin.[58]

Brace delighted in dialect. A professor of English, a determined amateur small-boat sailor, and an intensely patient man, he absorbed vocabulary and pronunciation, especially that used by children and the old. He loathed mass-media distortion, especially the corrupting of "northeast" into "nor'east," a pronunciation unknown along the New England coast, where alongshore locals say "nothe-east." In the easterly compass quadrants the same contraction obtains, but not in the westerly ones: thus "sou-west" still punctuates everyday speech, as it once governed the speech of sailing-ship helmsmen. Brace knew what Walt Whitman knew, that the speech of the people showcased and cloaked all manner of treasure.[59] But now as electronic media hasten the vocabulary standardization begun by public-school curricula and mass-circulation magazines, the ruin of words impedes all study of landscape, even casual inquiry into everything abandoned, grown over, pindling.

Old dictionaries consequently matter. Often they stand as ruins themselves. The second edition of *Webster's New International Dictionary* appeared in 1934, a year after the thirteen-volume *OED*. Massive and immediately authoritative in the United States, its 600,000 defined words spread across 3,400 pages. In 1961 appeared its successor, *Webster's Third New International Dictionary*: it had some 450,000 defined words, 100,000 of them new, in 2,726 pages. Its publisher dropped a quarter-million defined terms.[60] The 1934 dictionary can be acquired inexpensively, often for a pittance at estate and garage sales, and is worth lugging home or strapping to a bicycle carrier.[61] Anyone interested in vocabulary crucial in the study of women, African-Americans, farming (especially small-scale farming), household manufacturing, and other subjects Merriam-Webster editors deemed obsolescent in the late 1950s can profit from exploring it. Other old dictionaries, especially the multivolume *Century* ones published before 1915, prove valuable too, especially to anyone interesting himself or herself in landscape, especially landscape over time.

In 1837 Charles Richardson understood "landscape" as a nuanced word. Today his two-volume *New Dictionary of the English Language* makes most lexicographers chuckle if they deign to notice it at all. Richardson made frequent, glaring errors of etymology, and etymology entrances dictionary-makers and historians of lexicography: if remembered at all, he is remembered as a fierce enemy of Samuel Johnson.[62] But his dictionary sold well on both sides of the Atlantic, its usefulness—especially its definitions—infuriating Noah Webster yet satisfying British readers anxious for a dictionary more complete than Johnson's.[63] Richardson defined "landscape" as both a region and a country, and as something else: Richardson defined **landscape** as "a coast."[64]

A fertile field surrounded by thickly wooded hills, squared to spare fencing costs, smoothed by centuries of plowing, filled with light against the forest gloom. JRS

3 ECHOES

Once in a while landscape is new, fresh, almost virginal. South Georgia, the Falkland Islands, Kerguelen, the Crozets, Macquarie, Elephant, Pitcairn, and other islands, most in the South Polar Sea still so little noticed by news media and geography teachers, proved bereft of humans when Europeans discovered them. Unknown to humankind, not just to Europeans, they existed only as wilderness when found. Even today rare visitors and their few inhabitants (if any) point at little that is antique: settlement (if any) is too new.[1] But typically landscape is mature, often hoary, sometimes ancient, part prehistoric. Wilderness appears timeless.

Wilderness denotes the lair of beasts, where people go astray. Two Old English words, **wild** and **ness**, fuse, the former probably identifying deer and other game which lead on hunters, escape, and leave their pursuers lost. **Wild** later—certainly by the sixteenth century—connoted what it does today, anything in "a state of nature," lacking civilization, but ordinary people ignored philosophic nuance. They jumbled together undomesticated animals (what **beast** now typically connotes, unless the animal freights burdens) with newly met people unfamiliar with and sometimes scorning European protocols. Elizabethans termed such people **savages**, cheerfully misusing an Old French term derived from the Latin **silvaticus**, meaning people of the **silva**, the woods. No more pejorative to Romans than **rustic** is to Americans today, "silvaticus" emphasized the habitat of the savages rather than their behavior or seeming unintelligible language (the "bar-bar" that Romans heard and shaped into **barbarian**). Elizabethans conflated "savage" with **salvage**, a word rooted in the Latin term meaning "to save": Englishmen used the words interchangeably for a century or more, their linkages now ruins of nuanced understandings beyond encyclopedias. The Dry Salvages, exposed ledges off Cape Ann in Massachusetts and important in the poetry of T. S. Eliot (who summered near them as a boy), still pronounced "salwages" by locals, wrecked and still wreck mariners. While mariners might be saved and their vessels and gear salvaged, the name implies something beyond "barbarian" and the later **native**: some places might be savage rather than merely wild or might be wild but nonetheless succor or save or salvage those savaged at their margins.

Land here obstructs any acquaintance with wilderness, let alone essential landscape. Any inquiry into the meaning of the word involves what all mariners know: not all solid earth is land.

Oxford's *Dictionary of Environment and Conservation* defines "land" succinctly: "the solid, dry surface of the Earth, or any part of it. *Contrast* OCEAN."[2] Only one nautical dictionary defines the word. *Sailor's Word-Book: A Dictionary of Nautical Terms*, published in 1867 by retired Royal Navy admiral William Henry Smyth, implies something awkward: the term "in a general sense denotes *terra firma*, as distinguished from sea." But it comprehends some other solids as well. **Ledge**, for example, means "a compact line of rocks running parallel to the coast, and which is not unfrequently opposite sandy beaches. The north coast of Africa, between the Nile and the Lesser Syrtis, is replete with them."[3] Ledges might be submerged. Or not. Other nautical dictionaries sheer off from what Smyth confronted.

Earth or rock exposed at low tide never achieves the status of land, at least in the minds of seafarers. The shipwreck narrative beginning Daniel Defoe's early eighteenth-century *Robinson Crusoe* epitomizes the distinction. After a twelve-day storm, the master of a ship bound from Brazil to England determines to make for Barbados for repairs, endures another gale, and, blown far off course ("we were rather in danger of being devoured by savages than ever returning to our own country"), meets hazard. A lookout shouts "Land!" and the vessel strikes "upon a sand" and begins to break up; in what "might well be called *den wild zee*, as the Dutch call the sea in a storm," the men determine to land in a small boat. "We hastened our destruction with our hands, pulling as well as we could towards land," continues the narrator, for the boat oversets in the outer surf. Flung up on a sandbar momentarily dry, he recovers his senses only to be flung forward into deep water. Eventually, feeling "ground" with his feet, he stands up, runs islandward on the sandbar, and is swept up twice more until "the sea, having hurried me along as before, landed me, or rather dashed me, against a piece of rock," to which he holds until he marshals the will to run again. He struggles onto the beach exhausted, delirious with happiness at being alive, and then realizes he may be "devoured by wild beasts," which he assumes hunt by night, and so he climbs a tree, salvaged from drowning, on land, and in great danger still.[4] The next morning begins his landscape-making enterprise for which the novel (albeit often in abbreviated form) remains justly famous. Land can be shoveled, assembled, and otherwise improved from wilderness to landscape with some assurance of permanence.

Rock, ledges, and sandbars cannot. "Land ho!" announces either the anticipated appearance of land or the unantici-pated proximity of hazard. Icebergs provide one way of understanding what "land" means. Lookouts still shout "ice and breakers," not "land ho," when they see such. On a calm moonless night in a sea like glass, the lookouts on the *Titanic* missed the iceberg ahead because they looked for the white of breakers at the base of bergs: calm meant no surf, no visual warning. "Land ho" may mean sand or rock or coral endangering a vessel, but the cry does not mean "land" in the sense of earth that succors castaways. In *The Toilers of the Sea*, Victor Hugo thrashed out the significance of bits of rock exposed at the highest of high tides but nonetheless not true land because they offered no salvage to people wrecked on them, not even a depression filled with brackish water. He describes "a little promontory, rather of rock than land" to make clear its near uselessness; elsewhere he emphasizes that bare Norman Archipelago rocks "are rarely desert places," for smugglers, customs officers, crab-gatherers, and others rendezvous at them, unlike mid-ocean ones to which he devotes a chapter. No one lives on them: "no fruit trees are there, no pasturage, no beasts, no springs of water fitted for man's use." Castaways find only the briefest of respite if they survive surf and rocks: "This kind of rocks, which in the old sea dialect were called *Isolés*, are, as we have said, strange places. The sea is alone there; she works her own will."[5] If they get ashore, the best-equipped explorers can only tarry: rising surf, let alone storms, thrust them off. Such rocks resemble the tops of glaciers and other terrain permanently covered by ice. Much of Antarctica, for example, forces nuanced distinctions between topography and wilderness, surface and momentary human presence. On inshore and mid-sea rocks, castaways typically die of exposure: little is known of their perceptions. In the end, land is more than exposed rock. Land offers ordinary people the chance to inhabit. Hugo catalogs the geological realities of "promontories, forelands, capes, headlands, breakers, and shoals," but emphasizes too what "isolés" means in the steamship age. Freighters and liners give such perils wide berths, so wide most modern mariners never see them.[6]

Here two words matter. **Seascape** and **marine** designate paintings including the sea. In many cases, of course, the sea is the only subject, although painters often include the sky and birds, often gulls and albatrosses. A marine painting includes a ship or ships, maybe even a boat, now and then a castaway clinging to a spar or crate. Many marines depict naval actions and typically involve two or more vessels fighting, usually with cannon: but the genre includes modern warfare, even the contemporary destroyer on patrol. However much submariners insist that every seascape is a marine honoring their branch of naval service, a seascape may include rocks, ledges, and land alongshore, and for that matter littoral landscape marked by wharves, lighthouses, and other built form. Art historians dislike legalistic inquiry about whether the grounded or wrecked ship shifts the designation, but even astute schoolchildren now and then wonder how much land changes the artistic designation from seascape to landscape.[7] Part of any answer involves the connotations of land, including the legal term **dry land** and its younger if equally important sibling, **wetland**. Admiralty law, rarely noticed by landsmen, splinters quick answers: it inserts **sea state** into every discussion. Few art museum visitors think of Admiral Francis Beaufort's 1805 sea-conditions scale still used by mariners (Force Six, for example, designates winds between twenty-two and twenty-seven knots, indicated by waves eight to thirteen feet, whitecaps everywhere, dense spray). Art critics rarely define "sea state" either, nor do they write precisely about rocks, ledges, and other hazards especially dangerous in storms.

Rock devoid of vegetation offers only driftwood as potential fuel. Without driftwood (dry driftwood, preferably), castaways often die of exposure before perishing of thirst, let alone starvation. Taller rocks may offer shallow pools of brackish or guano-greened water, but people surviving surf often find only rock encrusted with salt. Nowhere is the importance of trees more vital in any definition of land than in the thinking of fishermen and other mariners working around pure rock, ice, and—more rarely—cooled lava.

Centuries-old mental images of so-called desert islands prove useful here. **Desert** denotes sand and aridity. **Deserted** connotes bereft of humans: sixteenth-century castaway narratives contracted and confused desertion into "desert." But contemporary Americans nonetheless think of desert islands as graced with freshwater (waterfalls especially) and lush vegetation, especially coconut palms (perhaps because into the 1940s many pronounced **dessert** as "dez-ert"). The sun beats down, warms the cold castaways, and life gets easy, à la Robinson Crusoe. No one thinks of hypothermia.

But they might think of savages, especially of cannibals. The whole tropically lush confusion harks back to hyped discovery reports, wishful thinking, islands Shakespeare populated with Prospero and Caliban, perhaps especially the Pacific Islands interrupting images filed mentally under "South Seas." Herman Melville charted the images even as he sharpened them in *Typee* (1846) and *Omoo* (1847), romantic reportage-fiction of deserting his whaling ship for cannibal lushness. A deserted beach is a romantic one now, and upscale vacationers hope to see no footprints other than their own. Unlike Robinson Crusoe, they expect no savages, only key lime pie or other dessert.

Ground which cannot itself sustain human life even for a few hours or days never truly achieves the status of land. Mariners call it **hazard** and avoid it. They and almost everyone else see it as something to avoid: scholars dismiss it with scant discrimination. **Landfall** designates the finding of land according to (or contrary to) navigational reckoning: seamen "make a landfall" when land, hopefully the intended coast, becomes visible on the horizon but is not yet recognized as a specific place. When it is identified precisely (in the words of H. G. Wells, when location has "risen from the blue indistinctness of the landfall"),[8] seamen speak still of "making land." In the terminology of ships' logbooks, the land is **made**. The usage connotes the conjuring of land from the sea (and the "mysteries" of navigation), the creating of it from water or larger vastness, the fall of light and the fall of mariners (the last used as in "the pirates fell on the merchant ship"). In civilized places built to welcome strangers, boats and ships arrive at piers, wharves, and other **landings** (even **staithes** or **hards**, mudbanks covered with sand or gravel so small boats may touch efficiently) fitted for the transfer of passengers and cargo. **Dock** designates the water adjacent to piers and other structures: even at low tide, depth of water must be such that vessels float, or else the bottom must be free of rocks and other hazards so they can "take the ground" without damage. "Touching bottom" while docked can be damaging, as can running aground: prudent mariners know landings as temporary havens only, places to rest but never to remain. Nautical usage informs the use of **landings** in architectural terminology: tall stairways have landings, typically every thirteen steps.

Away from navigable water **land** blossoms in age-old lushness. A four-letter word bearing an ancient history, it lately connotes—loosely—ground which supports habitation. But its derivations and meanings reward an ambit, however brief and rough.

From a Germanic root, **lando**, it arrived in Old English from the Old High German **lant** and Old Norse **land** by way of Old Frisian **land**. But it spread too as Old Celtic

landā into Breton as **lann**, Cornish as **lan**, Welsh as **llan**, and Old Irish as **lann**. If its roots are not further east than present-day Germany, it spread toward the Urals too. In Old Slavonic (known to lexicographers mostly in ecclesiastical documents) it became **lędina** and in Russian **lyada** or **lyadina**. From Russia it seems to have circled west, becoming in modern Swedish **linda**, a term lying atop the Old Norse **land**. All this matters, especially on summer Saturdays when suburbanites mow lawns.

In Britain collided the two streams of "land." The northern one designated most everything not sea and not freshwater, what lexicographers delineate by defining how mariners speak of it in "how the land lies" and other seaborne phrases. Essentially the word today designates the 55,000,000 square miles of earth surface not water, but it has many connotations. As Hugo and others note, alongshore, limicole language discriminates finely, in part because a second linguistic current infuses the northerly one. Old Celtic floats an understanding of land as enclosed space, a way of knowing Hugo discovered in the Norman Archipelago. It shapes contemporary Welsh and Irish: **llan** and **lann** identify enclosures, and in Wales **llan** sometimes means a churchyard or church building. But in Cornwall and further south, especially in Brittany, **lann** designates heath, and it is the root of the modern French word **lande**, which lexicographers understand as naming heath or moor, rather in the way the Russian **lyada** designates heath and **lyadina** desert. The modern Swedish overlay term means waste or fallow land. In modern Swedish, **mark** designates land. **Linda** names the wind. Looking for landmarks requires care,

especially in the currents of modern English so confused following the Norman landing in 1066.

Launde entered English from the Old French **launde**,
which designated "wooded ground" but not forest (something remarkably like **bosque** in northern New Spain). Four
hundred years after the Battle of Hastings, Englishmen
understood it to mean the interstices or openings in thinly
wooded terrain, a rough-edged near-synonym of **glade.** By
then the French used it to name open ground, probably
heathland, certainly not woods or forests. The history and
shape-shifting of **launde** illuminates any study of landscape,
because the word proved vibrant well into the eighteenth
century in its venerable spelling. **Lawn** means something
slightly different; its present orthography dates from the end
of the eighteenth-century, although educated Britons used
both spellings until about 1850.

Launde (and **laund**, the silent vowel dropped as the
word became in one way less important) and **lawn** remain
twisted in the etymological history of linen manufacture.
"Lawn as white as driven snow," sings Autolycus in *The
Winter's Tale* of linen especially white and especially expensive.[9] The word was known in English writing as early as
1415, and identified the rare cloth imported from Laon
(then spelled "Lan"), a small city northwest of Rheims. Producing pure-white cloth involved repeated washing, a process called **laundering**, but Englishmen created the term
willy-nilly from another, **lavendaring**, a word corrupted
from Latin root terms either for washing or for putting
sprigs of lavender in piles of folded linen, the plant itself
long before named as useful perfume for ladies' bathing

water. Linen manufacture developed slowly in England, powerful Englishmen coveted the imported cloth they called "lawn," and bishops and other ecclesiastics prized it before and after the Reformation. Sometimes the surplice sleeves of a vicar, but more usually those of a bishop, struck parishioners as the whitest cloth in the world. Ecclesiastics hoped such a response half-consciously focused parishioners on doctrines of theological purity. Today brides wear white for related reasons.

Here light illuminates lexicography. As "launde" became both the brilliant fabric of clergymen and greensward enclosed by forest, **glade** grew less used and its core meaning obscured by related terms.

Scandinavian roots run deep under the word, especially the Icelandic **glaðr**, denoting bright or shining. The root words designated an opening in a forest, a track cut through a dark forest, or a narrow, navigable channel (what **gutter** once meant in English marsh improvement terminology) dug through tall reeds, all of which accidentally admit light, something especially important to people knowing mostly dense coniferous woods and long winter twilight. Twentieth-century rural Swedes used **glad-yppen** to designate a lake totally free of ice, bright and shining in the spring sun: the dialect term resembles the Old English **glæd**, meaning shining, bright, and cheerful, and the later Dutch **glad**, bright, smooth, sleek, and German **glatt**, smooth, even, or polished. **Glad**, a word meaning happy, cheerful, and pleased, and **glade** share a common ancestry, only a fragment of which is the Latin **glaber**, meaning smooth, the *b* changing to *d* over time. Neither term owes much to the

Latin **gladius**, a sword, which survives in **gladiator**, although needed swords tend to be bright and shining. Light within larger dark is the core connotation of **glade**, even if relative.

So also is an element of natural process. "Farre in the forrest by a hollow glade" lives the wild man of Spenser's 1596 *The Faerie Queene*, a quintessential visual allegory often more illustrative of language in flux than Shakespeare's plays. While "a gloomy shade" governs ground beneath the shrubs, the glade is lighter than surrounding forest. No one made it. It is not the wet open ground designated by **lea** (**ley**, **lay**), a word rooted in the German **loh**, meaning a bog or morass (and also a wood or forest), nor is it arable (plowed) land planted to grass or left fallow for a while, called in English **lea** (**ley**, **lay**), rooted in the Old English **liegan**, "to lie," as in the phrase, "to lie fallow." However spelled, **lea** designates two different things, its meanings reach far into two wholly different roots, and it continually confuses British writers (and their readers). Both words help define **lawn**.

Lawns are typically sunny, dry, and appear so immediately. Appearance matters greatly. At the end of the eighteenth century, educated Britons used **laund** and **lawn** interchangeably, although by then the word denoted, according to the eighth edition of Samuel Johnson's *Dictionary* (1799), ecclesiastical linen and "an open area between woods." But British translation dictionaries emphasized the built character of the opening. In 1813 one translated the term into French as "une grande plaine dans un parc," a near-perfect plagiarizing of John Kersey's *New*

English Dictionary of 1702, "a plain in a Park." Lawns had become pleasure grounds, not for hunting but for strolling—and for looking at through windows.

Anyone might take in a lawn at a glance. Nothing occluded anything. Openness delighted and reassured. The casual and the lazy glanced and thought they understood it all, completely and perfectly. **Glance** denotes both a "swift dart of light" and a glimpse or hasty look, but as a verb it means too to graze, flash, or glide off or from. While **glare** is rooted in the Old English **glær**, naming amber but also influenced by Low German **glaren**, to glow (as amber does), **glance** comes from the Old French **glacier,** meaning to slip or glide. Lawns offer little chance of slipping. But lawns betray and "lawn" deserves more than a glance. By 1800 it designated part of what "land" (and "laund") denoted two centuries earlier, a more or less enclosed, open, dry, sunny area surrounded by trees. "Land" no longer connoted what **landā** had in Old Celtic, what **lann** designates in Ireland, enclosed open space.

By about 1700, "land" designated all dry ground that might support prolonged habitation, a usage the English had accepted as early as 900, in *Beowulf.* Vestiges of the other usage survive. In England between about 1450 and 1900, "land" identified a single structure divided into flats (each legally a house) presided over by its owner or a deputy: why the owner (and often manager) of a structure is called **landlord** or **landlady** puzzles contemporary tenants. The deep explanation involves the obsolescent understanding of land not only as discrete, enclosed ground but ground owned by one person and divided among several (or many) inhabitants. But such inquiry leads only into lawns. Land comprises far more than lawns (what survives in Old England as **greensward**, the green skin of earth), and lawyers know it.

Lawyers still follow precedent dating to the Battle of Hastings (1066) and the subsequent Norman Conquest, now and then sorting Norman veneer from Old English common law. While Parliament under Edward III mandated three centuries later that trials and pleadings be conducted in English (most ordinary Englishmen spoke no French, which they understood as the tongue of the invader, noble or not), well into the seventeenth century clerks, lawyers, and jurists kept all records in Norman, what lexicographers know as **law French**.[10] Not until 1650 did Parliament require that English supplant Norman in all documents.[11] Late in the fifteenth century, Thomas Littleton, a judge committed to limiting the authority of kings, produced the first English-language textbooks for aspiring lawyers: hitherto students learned only from lectures given in Latin. Two centuries later, Edward Coke authored his four-volume *Institutes of the Laws of England*, a detailed but broad survey of English common law as influenced by Norman and post-Norman statute, by Littleton, and by hundreds of judicial decisions publicly reported.[12] What law students now learn as "Coke upon Littleton" shapes law, points of law, and modern legal lexicography: "Land, in the most general sense, comprehends any ground, soil, or earth whatsoever; as meadows, pastures, woods, moors, waters, marshes, furzes, and heath. Co. Litt.4a" runs the definition in *Black's Law Dictionary*, which boasts of defining "terms and phrases of

American and English Jurisprudence, Ancient and Modern."
English and American law understands an elastic definition,
everything from "the solid material of the earth" to ground
inhabited permanently, year round, by people living in permanent structures. But elasticity still stretches back to the
Norman.

Most Americans discover fragments of all this only
when they buy land or land under a house, or land, house,
and **appurtenances**, "as a right of way or other easement to
land; an out-house, barn, garden, or orchard, to a house or
messuage." **Messuage** staggers any first-time "home buyer,"
for it harks back to the Norman French understanding that
a house alone proves rather useless: a "landed family" needed
a barn, stable, chicken coop, and other structures to store
and process crops and shelter livestock. Contemporary
jurists note that in American usage it means "dwelling
house," a stance which only confuses buyers who ask why
the French term follows the English words (or at least
"house") and so ought to mean something else, even if only
slightly different.[13] In the process of "passing papers,"
buyers, especially young buyers excited to be acquiring their
first home, momentarily confront the mysteries implicit in
definitions of land and landownership, but only if they read
the words and wonder at what seems pure verbiage, and
Norman verbiage at that. Few do. Few ponder the similar
but different roots of **law** (from the Old Norse **lag**, something laid, laid down, permanent) and **statute** (from the
Latin, something set, stationed, standing) and so miss the
enduring, fitful fusing of Old English and Norman legal
bases. Most glance at attorneys and then sign, not clear at all

about appurtenances and messuages, unwary of mysteries of home, home land, homeland security, not clear about real estate, not clear at all about language recorded for eternity, happily excited about rooms and windows and lawns, not clear about owning land, land hopefully dry, so excited that they miss the lexicographical portal on **land**.

But they will not miss the importance of mowing and fertilizing their front lawn, of painting house and picket fences, of maintaining their real estate as they hope neighbors will maintain theirs. If things go wrong in the neighborhood, if wilderness somehow intrudes, they can move, but they cannot easily move their house and cannot move their land. Land is fixed albeit subject to all sorts of vicissitudes. In the eyes of the law, "land" names something peculiarly real.

Movable, trailed over trails, the mass-produced mobile home whispers still of old animosity toward cottages erected overnight. JRS

4 HOME

Home buyers often leave banks or law offices stunned at having borrowed vast sums to be repaid over thirty years, excited about their new homes, and uninterested in legalities. They turn to some place new, sometimes brand-new, more often old but new to them. Few think about arcane vocabulary. But underneath their excitement thrives one bit of English (and American) common law, a bit that takes root when they occupy their new house, and it grows around them like a vine. Everyone who owns a house knows that "a man's home is his castle." While codified generally in the Declaration of Independence and in the Constitution, the phrase flourishes in things deeper, the core language of the common law and sand castles on a summer beach.

Once the deed (and typically the mortgage) are registered at the appropriate courthouse, the buyers turn to their new residence. Properly (and legally), they **attorn**. The word comes from the Latin root meaning "to turn," although by the Norman invasion it meant "to prepare" as well, perhaps "to turn aside to prepare" or "to turn to another." It meant and still means (even legally) "to shift homage," either because a lord has died or because a free adult has chosen another nobleman to honor and obey, even if only temporarily. **Lawyer** retains in its spelling the centuries-old form of "ier," a noun suffix denoting someone who does: but while **carrier** and **glazier** use the modern spelling (and have for centuries, as **brazier**, a term no longer used for one who brazes, suggests), the legal term retains an older one connoting an agent who does things, usually thought bad, to people, especially the poor. **Attorney** retains an old spelling too, but connotes something post-Norman, someone to whom one turns, temporarily, for help. Certainly the attorney is deputized by the one in need of advice or other assistance, but after deputizing, the client follows attorney instruction precisely. An attorney goes to court and defends the client. Something about a knight helping the wronged still illuminates the word, something absent from its seeming synonym, something still illuminating class (Shakespeare's Dick the Butcher espouses revolt by screaming "kill the lawyers," not "kill the attorneys") and fairy-tale need for knights in shining armor.[1]

One way or another, transfer of real property involves visiting court, going to the courthouse to register a deed and often a **mortgage**. Originally from the Latin, **mortuum vadium**, a "dead pledge," the word defined a conveyance of land in payment of a debt: having transferred the land, the grantor acknowledged that the debt (and any interest in the land) henceforth was dead to him. Subsequently it shifted meaning, after the Normans reorganized the law, to mean a conveyance in which the one acquiring land promised to repay by a certain time a debt, either in goods (crops), money, or service, especially military. The promise (often manifested in a promissory note) over time became heritable, something the acquirer might pass on to heirs after death: but even as the word acquired "gage," the newer Norman term for "pledge," the fundamental concept obtained. So long as the acquirer paid regularly (or irregularly, if the promise involved service in time of war), the transfer was dead to the conveyor. **Real estate** thus means land and everything annexed to it naturally (grass, trees, ponds, and so on) and by artifice (orchards, sluices, houses, barns, and so on): jurisprudence further defines "everything" as "houses and appurtenances, messuages" and **hereditaments**. Not only does the purchaser of land (or real estate) own until death what he has bought, he owns the right to will it to his heirs—and he owns the right and privilege to pay homage to a lord—nowadays (in the United States) a representative government elected by voters and in peacetime requiring only taxes.

All of this proves consequential in any study of landscape. Contemporary law is deeply rooted in land and in the ownership of land. Any apartment renter arrested for a serious crime and bound over for trial must post cash bail; those without savings accounts often borrow money from bail bondsmen. But an owner of real estate, of land, need only sign a form pledging the holding against flight. Everyday American speech emphasizes something all too easily missed. Renters pay taxes indirectly through landlords, but homeowners pay taxes directly (sometimes attached to monthly mortgage payments). When a road needs fixing or trash pickup becomes irregular, the former complain but the latter demand their rights as taxpayers, never as citizens. Common law and custom distinguish between renters (even those with leases), who can move quickly away from problems, and landowners, who have deep stakes in a defined, bounded, surveyed place. The former may coalesce into **mobs** (attractive to Dick the Butcher), a word Britons contracted from **mobile**: the **mobility** may surge through streets, damaging property owned by landowners rooted in place. Land lines, however less common by the year, connect to telephones ringing in fixed places, not just anywhere, phones unlikely to facilitate and organize riot, phones election-year pollsters love. When mobs surge, landowners summon police, knights in blue, **attercops**, cops who act in the role of medieval **sheriffs** (from the Old English **scīr-gerēfa**, **shire reeve**, he who reeves or threads or ties together a shire, mostly by collecting rents due the monarch, but also by weaving webs to catch criminals) or **grieves** (similar in sound, and probably corrupted from the Latin **gravare** meaning burden or grief, what tax collectors often bring). Sheriffs, constables, process servers, and cops prosper with counties and shires, in New Hampshire and elsewhere, serving as arms of the court and in rural (traditional) New England serving alongside elected or appointed hog reeves, wardens of dams, and other officers medieval Englishmen recognized as minor officers of the crown stitching together legal form and landscape.

Almost never did officers enter a man's home without a warrant. Warrants proved hard to get, local magistrates demanding probable cause, witnesses, perhaps some solid, tactile, real evidence, something more definite than attercop suspicion. Neighbors (and centuries later, firefighters) might enter to extinguish fire, but otherwise royal officers needed warrants. Even today, landlords enter properties almost at will, to change smoke detector batteries and repair leaking plumbing (especially when leaks come through ceilings in apartments below), but police officers must still obtain warrants. None of this is legal nit-picking. Sand castles recall fundamental concepts in English common law.

Owning real estate, even looking at it intelligently, means confronting reality and realms, recognizing the role of near-absolute power in ordering and maintaining any landscape.

Power originates in might, armed might, might that may conquer an area of ground and impose its will on the conquered but must defend its area against enemies without and within. Castles exemplify armed might. In them resides the power of shaping, maintaining, and discipline. In the castle courtyard on summer days, in the great hall in winter, assembles power and those approaching it. In the castle is court.

No matter what sort of government suffuses a place— theocracy, plutocracy, communism, aristocracy, military, oligarchy, monarchy, autocracy, ochlocracy (rule by the mob), or timocracy (rule by property owners only)—core power keeps the sewer and water supply systems operating, public transit running, post offices moving mail, and other so-called basic services functioning. Ochlocracy fails rapidly at the task, but most other types prove more or less efficient because they must or face rebellion or dissolution or conquest. Adherents (especially proselytizers) of specific forms of government routinely ignore the similarities of landscape from one regime to another. Almost all forms of government support fire and police departments, defense against external enemies, road building and maintenance, energy delivery, and public health departments dealing with drinking water, sewerage, garbage disposal, and other important issues.

No matter what the regime, morning commuters who board trains and buses at terminals distant from city centers usually find seats, and often they find seats for the last few stops in the evening. Bridges over which trains and buses pass must support the vehicles. Tracks and roads must be passable, however imperfect. From one regime to another, laws of physics govern the railroad and highway gradients, the curvature of routes, the pitch of sewer pipes, and countless other facets of engineering, building, and maintenance. Travelers interested in urban design, canal siting, open-pit mining, power line location, highway traffic signaling, and similar subjects find occasional innovation but a remarkable similarity in design, construction, and maintenance no matter what the form of government. Successful physical (especially mechanical) innovation passes rapidly across regimes: heads of civil departments routinely convene to exchange information about what they term "best practice." Military leaders may be less circumspect than fire chiefs anxious to know how to extinguish chemical fires, but they too learn quickly from each other. No matter its nationality, an aircraft carrier turns into the wind to launch and recover aircraft. That is the best way, best practice.

Some power must order an area for complexity to develop, prosper, and endure. Thomas Hobbes's 1651 *Leviathan, or the Matter, Forme, and Power of a Common Wealth Ecclesiasticall and Civil* explicates the concept in terms of monarchy, aristocracy, and democracy, arguing that government for the highest, greatest good proves impossible because people bicker constantly over what the good might be. Hobbes argues instead that government originates in each individual's fear of violent, untimely death and in the basic selfishness (even wickedness) of each individual if left wholly unrestrained. However grim his argument, Hobbes's insistence that all groups of people must live in orderly ways proves fierce. Some power must guarantee continuous freedom from assault, battery, and murder and—by extension—the right to feed and clothe oneself and one's family, to maintain property, to perpetuate landownership. Any observer of landscape, perhaps the landscape which attracts so many tourists to rural Britain, must ponder the long arm of *Leviathan*.

In larger castles lived (at least sometimes) counts, barons, dukes, and other noblemen descended from those who once governed (more or less absolutely) miniature realms in time amalgamated into proto-nation-states ruled by kings who more or less conquered lesser competitors. Fairy-tale images notwithstanding, the castles spread across early England (and what became France, Germany, and other nations) morphed into local loci of larger (typically royal and national) military and civil order. In times of invasion, crusade, or other military need, local noblemen paid homage to their monarch in more than taxes collected from yeomen and peasants; they provided soldiers more or less professional. In peace they kept the peace, their men-at-arms, eventually sheriffs, identifying and capturing highwaymen, burglars, and other criminals. But in England the most powerful of the regional nobles combined to limit the power of the king.

The Magna Carta of 1215 endures in legal history and schoolroom lessons as the first formal restraint placed upon a monarchy. At Runnymede, a great meadow, the barons defined the power of King John: no longer could he rule arbitrarily, twenty-five of the barons might nullify his proclamations, his mercenaries had to leave England, and so on. Above all, no Englishman might be punished outside the established law. Two years later the barons accomplished something equally important.

The Charter of the Forest chiefly concerns ordinary people, the freemen (not serfs) of the realm, in relation to the natural resources. King John had swept more and more land into his personal royal forests to the detriment of stability, industry, and property. "Henceforth every freeman, in his wood or on his land that he has in the forest, may with impunity make a mill, fish preserve, pond, marl-pit, ditch or arable in cultivated land outside coverts, provided that no injury is thereby given any neighbor," asserts one of the crucial clauses. Imposed on John's son, Henry III, the Charter of the Forest asserts specific rights necessary to the ordinary agricultural and other property-owning enterprises of ordinary English families. Merged into the Magna Carta eighty years later in the so-called Confirmation of Charters, the Charter of the Forest obtained in English law until 1972, when Parliament modernized it in an act defending wild creatures and natural land.[2]

Legal nuances and practical history notwithstanding, both charters became important in the early seventeenth-century Puritan revolt. Hobbes's argument was shaped by the civil war that preceded the beheading of Charles I and the interregnum under Cromwell, and in turn shaped the subsequent precise understanding throughout Britain that Parliament and the restored monarchy (under Charles II and subsequently) ruled subject to the law, and that Eng-lishmen enjoyed widespread, specific rights, which (however vaguely) extended to Englishmen resident in colonies.[3] In the heavily forested thirteen colonies, the Charter of the Forest echoed loudly, as did Hobbesian assertion. Power, military and civil, must keep colonists safe from violent death at the hands of Native Americans, the French, and pirates, and must protect their livelihood and property, especially their houses and improved land. Otherwise, most colonists understood, leviathan (the government) seemed almost unnecessary.

In the centuries after the Confirmation of Charters, castles signified both the reach of royal authority and the loci of forces limiting that authority, but chiefly they announced the power of order. In the castle resided the power that kept the king's peace, the peace of the market-place, the order of highways (and hopefully lesser roads and cart paths), the safety of all people (especially women and children), and the inviolate sanctity of real estate. When needed, power sallied forth from the castle toward disorder and wickedness. At times knights and bailiffs and sheriffs carried some identifying accessory, usually a sword but sometimes a staff. When juries are brought to the scene of a crime, contemporary Americans find a bailiff with a staff, its verticality momentarily marking ordinary space temporarily transformed into a court: when courts exhaust jury pools, bailiffs go out to the city sidewalks, maces raised, and order citizens in to duty. Most of the time castles belong in fairy tales (or on beaches) or in the sets of films featuring princesses, motion pictures which prompt little girls to dress as princesses, causing adults to smile and rare savants to wonder if the girls grow up counting on knights, in shining armor and otherwise, to rescue them when necessary.

But as Coke noted in a verdict at the foundation of the common law, "a man's house is his castle," a phrase that necessarily concerns any inquirer into landscape.[4]

It does *not* mean that a man can do as he pleases within his own walls. He cannot murder himself or his wife and children, for example, nor may he set fire to his house. Never has the concept meant such.

It means the house stands barred against illegal entry, including that of the king. It is a safe refuge from all outside it. Especially it is safe for babies and children. And it means something else, frequently mangled in journalistic prose.

It means house.

As house buyers find if they read paperwork handled mostly by attorneys, **house** is not **home**. A house is permanent. Home is otherwise, sometimes merely where the heart is, where a hat hangs, a favorite term of American real estate agents since the 1920s. In the United Kingdom such professionals call themselves "estate agents."

Here Norman (or law French) proves remarkably resilient and meaningful.[5] **Messuage** often appears in deeds, meaning usually **dwelling house** but sometimes (and to precise, well-educated attorneys and surveyors caught up in title disputes) structures and space within the **curtilage**, the fence and walls most intimately enclosing a house, barn, and other buildings. What New Englanders designate by **farmstead** and High Plains ranchers call (inside courthouses) **ranch** varies across the United States, but everywhere English common law obtains, "messuage" (probably from the Old French **ménage** meaning "family," but with connotations of domestic animals too, at least the trained ones, as **menagerie** connotes) denotes a house and its near outbuildings. In many parts of England (and in Europe and much of Asia), a structure housing a family (including an extended one, often with servants) extends more or less around a courtyard with stables, pigsties, dovecotes, henhouses, and other buildings sheltering animals, and often granaries and hay barns. A close fence keeps toddlers and animals from straying and excludes foxes and other predators, and perhaps excludes strangers, who must shout, knock, or ring for entry. A court (from the Latin **cors**, a court, by way of the Old French **cortillage**, **curtilage**) connotes both intimacy and enclosure, concepts expressed in the Old English **geard** and its cognates Old Frisian **garda** and Old Norse **gard**. From this root blossomed two traditional, important English words, **garden** and **yard**, near-synonyms now but separated in usage by the Atlantic.

Well after the Norman Conquest, **court** (designating an enclosed place, not the castle and retinue of the sovereign or lesser noble) fused with **yard**, producing **courtyard**, which properly means the accessory structures and outdoor space of a rural house. While sometimes applied to inns (distinguished from taverns by renting rooms to travelers staying overnight) and eventually to hotels, **courtyard** emphasizes the domestic meaning of **yard**. Many yards, especially fenced-off areas of construction, have no inhabitants: people live elsewhere than in lumber yards, stockyards, boatyards, and railroad yards. Houses have yards, especially in the countryside where the yard is a place of work usually involving animals. Over centuries, especially in the United States, structures sheltering vehicles, vessels, equipment, and small children came to be understood as houses, as in **firehouse**, **boathouse**, **head house** (sheltering mining machinery, especially winding gear), and **schoolhouse**: late in the twentieth century the suffix changed to **station**, as in **fire station**, a designation so new it is still two words. Legally and in traditional speech, even precise ordinary British and American writing, **house** designates something special and stolidly enduring, especially after dark.

Burglary offers a way into knowing houses as critical components of landscape. From the Old German **burgus** designating a fortified place (borrowed into Old French as **bourg**, a village), producing **burg** in German urban place names and **borough** in English, a town (not necessarily walled) governed by property owners called **burgesses** (a word known in American schoolrooms only as naming the colonial Virginia legislature), "burglary" means breaking and entering in the nighttime, particularly into a house. In older English **hamesecken**, it was and remains an unnerving, revolting crime heavily punished. Burglary involves stealth, penetration, and defilement of honest people properly asleep in bed. In his *Commentaries on the Laws of England*, William Blackstone emphasizes that the circumstances of a householder waking to discover a burglar "leave him this natural right of killing the aggressor," and that the law "tenders [such] a regard to the immunity of a man's house, that it styles it his castle and will never suffer it to be violated with impunity." Blackstone emphasizes that other crimes piggyback on burglary, especially eavesdropping and arson, and that a man may assemble as many as eleven other men to safeguard his house without being accused of "raising a riot, rout or unlawful assembly." Entering an open door or window proves mere trespass, especially if done by day, but crawling down chimneys is burglary. Breaking into a barn or warehouse or "houses where no man resides" must be punished less harshly, for such is not "attended with the same circumstances of midnight terror." But if the warehouse be "appurtenant" to the house, its burglary is the same as if the house itself is burgled: so also is burglary of a church and houses from which occupants are temporarily away.[6] By the middle of the eighteenth century Blackstone and his predecessors had a massive body of statute and case law defining everything from "after dark" (when one man could not see another's face to identify him, something a full moon did nothing to change) to eliminating fair booths and upturned carts (covered with canvas or not) from the structures subject to burglary law. Entering such meant mere thievery.

Arson also preoccupied English and Scottish jurists. The oldest English laws punished arson, especially of a house or crop, with incineration. Under Henry VI, Parliament made arson high treason (the only crime the United Kingdom still punishes by death is arson in Her Majesty's dockyards), but Parliament under Edward VI reduced it again to a felony, though one in which the condemned lacked benefit of clergy. Unlike burglary, arson had the potential to ignite more than one house, to set alight entire villages, even towns and cities. A communicable and thus especially heinous crime worried a nation living in thatched-roof houses.

Always **house** appears in post-Conquest statutes and commentaries, often as **mansion house**, an enduring term from Norman. **Mansion** comes from the Latin **mansio**, meaning a staying, via the French **manere**, the root of **manor** and **permanent**. "House" comes from the Old English and Old Frisian **hūs**, itself related to an ancient, Gothic word meaning temple or god-house, **gudûs**. But lexicographers know little of its ultimate origin, some arguing that it came from the Aryan **keudh** and **hud**, verbal roots meaning a hiding or hideout, a place to hide. Ancient and darkly verbal, still alive in an English dialect plural form, **housen**, different from the twelfth-century plural, **husas**, the term denotes a secure, permanent family living place, a place to hide securely (even while asleep) from the weather, nighttime predators, nuisance neighbors, and in some ways at least, from monarchy itself.

Hobbes understood the need to hide peacefully from absolute power and that power survived best when privacy protected the people from it. Houses prove critical in any understanding of liberty and freedom in British legal thinking. Legally, culturally, and emotionally, "house" connotes far more than shelter from bad weather or cold. Houses store food and firewood to enable independent, long-term withdrawal from the public realm, for example, or to entertain unexpected guests. Only rarely do university students learn much about the folklore associated with houses, say the ancient and enduring folktale of the family surprised by their cold, hungry, rain-soaked king, the monarch the family invites inside, into a private realm nonetheless fitted for him.

Dwelling designated something else, a mean and provocative otherness post-Conquest jurists struggled to marginalize. **Dwelling** originates in the Old English **dwela**, a going astray, wandering, erring, or deceit, similar to Old Norse and Old High German words for tarrying. At the beginning of the thirteenth century it had begun to mean staying, remaining, or living for a while in a place but not permanently. Over centuries it evolved into connoting a permanent residence, what English common law emphasizes in **dwelling house**, a term codifying what **mansion house** meant to the Norman nobility. Especially in the American colonies and in the new republic, **dwelling** morphed into **cabin**, especially **log cabin**, one product of making landscape, and citizens in cabins, even squatters, acquired most of the rights of householders. At first glance it seems easy to dwell too long on such nuances.

But **dwelling** illuminates the fundamental difference between a house and less permanent structures, some erected illegally. A house is permanent, difficult to move, certainly impossible to move quickly or in a clandestine way, such as after dark. Its ownership and occupation confer and announce status. In it a man becomes a **husband** and, assuming he farms, a **yeoman**: a woman married to him marries the house too, and so becomes a **housewife**. Both hold the house across time and reinforce the stability announced by castles, monarchy, and the common law, all of which is good, and confers titles: Goodman and Goodwife, the latter sometimes contracted to "Goody," as in the long-lived "Goody Two-Shoes." If he farms his own land about the house, the husband becomes not only a **husbandman**, husbanding the earth itself, but a yeoman, a commoner beneath the rank of gentlemen but entitled to serve on juries, bring his longbow to battle, and—far earlier than most suspect—elect the knights of the shire.[7] Husband, householder, yeoman … voter. Dwelling connoted rather less.

In 1588 Parliament passed "An Acte Againste Erectinge and Mayntayninge of Cottages," forbidding anyone to erect a cottage unless he owned or leased four acres of ground. The Act exempts shelters erected by miners and quarrymen, shepherds, woodsmen, and keepers of game in forests. It explicitly exempts cottages "made within a Myle of the Sea, or upon the syde of suche parte of any Navigable River where the Admyrall ought to have jurisdiction" so long as sailors or men "of manual occupation" (chiefly boatbuilders) erect and live in them.[8] Toward the close of the sixteenth century, poor men with families had begun to erect cottages, often mere huts, overnight on village common land used mostly for grazing. Flimsy at first, such cottages became more permanent by the day and vexed local authorities, who understood them as appropriating land without payment, interfering with established agrarian practices, and offering nuisance.

Cottage comes from the Old English **cot**, a hut. **Hut** is kin to the Old High German **hutta**, meaning "to conceal" or "that which conceals," and is probably a variant of **house**, but it can also refer to a tangled, matted knot in a sheep's fleece, perhaps from the Middle Latin **cottus**, meaning "a quilt." **Cot** is a tricky word. In Hindi it designates the simple, makeshift bed British colonists discovered in India, but now in English it connotes something less than a bed (or bedstead), certainly one more movable. The Dutch word **husk** plays a role here: originally designating a diminutive house, it soon fused with the Old English **hosa** meaning "a case": an ear of corn, snug in its husk, is nonetheless snug in something much less sound than the shell of a nut.[9] By the late sixteenth century, many British householders considered cottages suspect: often erected of flimsy material in the forest or at the edge of common fields, they hid families or groups of unrelated people, something lingering in the word **coterie**. A century later the word connoted more sound structures housing weavers, poor people working with wool and owning no land, paying pittance rent to landlords. When mines gave out or tree felling ended, workers abandoned cottages and moved on. Unless runaway serfs or other masterless people moved into them, cottages collapsed quickly. Only at the seaside did cottages endure, often being repaired or replaced after great storms, inhabited by poor men more focused on fishing boats and other vessels than on the quality of family shelter. The 1588 act thus lies at the heart of suspicion and dislike.

All sorts of squatters, especially tramps, sometimes erect flimsy shelters on land they do not own and, having little to lose, may assemble in mobs and rampage, as Hobbes insisted they would if established power failed to restrict them. Campers, trailers, mobile homes, converted school buses, automobiles, and similar shelters worry the establishment, the stable, the ones who pay property tax levied on permanent houses surrounded by yards, who view drifters with narrowed eyes, who see them sponging on services for which they do not pay.[10] Those who live in houses read "The Three Little Pigs" to their young children, noting that wolves at doors and failures made of straw reinforce ancient certainties and dislikes.

Fireplaces and chimneys distinguished houses from cottages until well into the seventeenth century. In the late thirteenth century, wealthy Englishmen began abandoning the great-hall central fireplace that sent smoke upward through a hole in the roof. After prolonged experiment with wattle-and-daub chimneys, English householders moved toward stone or brick hearths and—typically—brick chimneys, something accomplished only around 1720.[11] Not only did the chimneys require substantial timber framing around them, the masonry proved a further, massive statement of permanence. Hearth and chimney anchored the house and screamed of stability. Cottagers (**cotters** in Scotland) retained the medieval open fire and roof hole. Statute and case law adapted smoothly: crawling down a chimney open to the sky is burglary nonetheless.[12]

Only at the seacoast do cottages delight householders vacationing from responsibility. Usually simple and cheerfully cramped (though sometimes ostentatious mansions), cottages stand open to summer wind and tracked-in sand. Great gales may damage or destroy them, but their very impermanence delights and rewards because the impermanence stands proudly open to view. Only rarely do cottages hide. Typically the seacoast is open, full of light, inviting gaze, even if cottages stand close together in haphazard, cheerful lack of privacy and some visitors sleep on cots or on floors. In summer all is fun, and sunlight blinds. In winter, cold and wind pierce uninsulated walls and surf encroaches. Out-of-season visitors know that cottages prove temporary, are scarcely attached to the ground, and exist at the pleasure of King Neptune, not the law of castles and courts. Winter criminals break, enter, and steal: they do not burgle. In winter, cottages stand bleak and shabby, causing shudder, not satisfying.

Not stable.

Only now and then do visitors smitten with sunlit beaches note how the sand drifts and shifts around and under cottages, that few cottages boast lawns, that cottages lack yards.

Beneath its windbreak, snug on its south-facing slope, the farmstead in its fields exemplifies accretionary construction over time, all an adaptation to family and farming change, planning, and onset of winter. JRS

5 STEAD

Always more than a house, the American suburban home epitomizes small-scale landscape making and maintenance. Its whole reveals the deep power of being established, living in place, being stable, living in light.

John Brinckerhoff Jackson (1909–1996) noted the ubiquitous components of that whole, the front lawn and back yard, the small vegetable garden, the fruit tree (bearing or ornamental), the boundaries, fenced or hedged. His seminal article "Ghosts at the Door" appeared in 1951 in *Landscape* magazine, a journal he founded and edited for decades as a private effort to direct the attention of educated people to the vernacular or common landscape, something he hesitated to define simply. Then and still, educated people often scorn suburban landscape as reflecting homogeneity and blandness, if not lack of originality and intellectual depth. Against it they array the seeming excitement and cultural diversity of cities, the intellectual rigor of architect-designed structure, the spaces created by landscape architects, the complex, nuanced verbiage of design critics. In subway stations and elsewhere they whistle in their own dark.

"Loyalty to a traditional idea of how the world should look is something which we not always take into account when analyzing ourselves or others," Jackson asserted of something fundamental in any examination of any landscape. "Yet it is no more improbable than loyalty to traditional social or economic ideas or to traditional ideas in art."[1] Here tradition proves powerful. Tradition underlies the deep veneer of modern culture. Children should be safe. Public water and sewerage systems should work efficiently. Accused are innocent until proven guilty by juries of their peers. A wife cannot testify against her husband. Certainly tradition inveigles and puzzles, especially in charged moments. Highly educated, glass-ceiling-smashing young women often still wear something borrowed and something blue at their weddings, and their fathers often still respond to clergymen asking who gives the women to be wed. The same women pass their eighteenth birthday free of the Selective Service mandate that men reaching that age register for military service. Dogs wear collars displaying licenses. Cats do not.

Domestic cats came late to western Europe and Britain, some varieties perhaps brought home by the first crusaders. Witches nursed familiars long before, of course: ravens and bats, hedgehogs and other creatures connected them with Old Religion force. **Cat** "is common European of unknown origin," rooted in Latin and classical Greek, opines the *Oxford English Dictionary*, noting that no form "is preserved in Gothic." Primary gender varies according to country. In

Old Irish, **cat** is masculine, but in Welsh and Cornish **cath** is feminine, all perhaps from the masculine Old Norse **kött**; the Spanish **el gato** translates as **die Katze** in German. (The Romance forms of the word probably derive from the late Latin **cattus**.) *Felis domesticus* proved cause for suspicion, even among lexicographers. As late as 1527 one author remarked bluntly that "the mouse hunter or catte is an onclene beste & a poison ennemy to all myce," perhaps distinguishing it from the British wild cat and also from the male or he-cat, the tomcat kept to kill rats, and implying its antipathy to cuddling.[2] Cats bite, startle, and star in a constellation of superstitions, many involving nighttime, pantries, crossroads, devils, and misadventure. They wander at will through neighborhoods, subsidized predators devouring toads, feeder-fed birds, butterflies, snakes, and baby bunnies, crossing boundaries at will, tormenting watchdogs from afar, and emphasizing traditional loathing of the mice and rats which consume food stocks and carry disease. Of all the creatures Halloween aficionados celebrate annually, they invite only cats—sometimes—into their beds.

Tradition intrigues and seduces. Like cats it sometimes bites or scratches. It disturbs modernists, especially those who hope to modernize those they condemn as backward, antiprogressive perhaps, stuck in their ways, conservative. After hearing the modernist pitch, conservatives all too often offer alternatives, usually following the word **instead**. Instead of urban high-rise apartment buildings, why not houses in large-lot suburbs?

Jackson insisted that the landscape most Americans cherish is that of northwestern Europe: "Whatever the ethnic origin of the individual American, however long his family may have lived in this country, we are descendants, spiritually speaking, of the peoples of Great Britain and Ireland, of the Low Countries, and to a lesser extent of northern France and western Germany."[3] In 1951 the assertion struck some as broad and arrogant. Many decades later it irritates some more deeply, in part because it explains a cherished landscape constituent and a devoted, even fierce allegiance to it, one for which individuals and families sacrifice, one rooted in the common law and crypto-religious fealty. Its roots extend to great calamity too, more dimly and more deeply rooted than the calamity of Friday, October 13, 1307.[4] Suburbanites mow lawns to forestall its return.

Indeed, specters lurk outside the doors of suburban homes. Momentarily glimpsed, maybe at twilight by commuters leaving and returning, they prove tangible, touchable, real beyond argument.

In front, an essentially unused lawn represents the meadow of a medieval freehold. Kept free of people (particularly romping children) and especially animals, it exists to make hay. And it is mowed regularly, if not with a scythe, although its harvest is discarded or composted.

Behind the house, out back, lies the back yard, part farmyard, part pasture. There children and domesticated animals, dog and cat, roam. No goats or cows or sheep chomp the grass now, but typically it grows enclosed, inside fences, not exposed to public view like the lawn out front, made safe from predators, animal and otherwise.

In some sunny corner flourishes or languishes a small vegetable garden, planted in hope and tomatoes every spring and abandoned or turned under every autumn. It represents the plowed fields of long ago, tilled earth, arable land.

Near it (sometimes shading it) grows a self-pollinating apple or pear tree, or maybe an ornamental flowering cherry. Momentarily beautiful in spring, the tree sometimes produces fruit, edible, maybe better in jams and pies, but often harvested by squirrels and chipmunks. Perhaps it is pruned, if only rarely and haphazardly. The tree memorializes the orchard of times before.

Minor constituents recall fragments. The potted herbs recall the housewife's herb garden once planted for medicinal and culinary use, the compost pile recalls the manure heap, and bird houses recall dovecotes (**dovecote** connoting a diminutive form of **cottage**). A few shade trees mark the memory of the woodlot, the source of building timber and critical winter fuel, and the garage (now often amalgamated into the house in a most medieval way) whispers of barns and stables, of things stored. Flowers emphasize an innate need for beauty, blooms to adorn church altars, the slivers of color and scent housewives prized in dooryards where they worked outside in sunshine and warmth.

All of this matters in traditional, inchoate ways. All of it opens on the history of landscape.

But all of it matters in an unsettling way too. No other built form adapts more easily to change, especially fundamental change, than the large-lot suburban home. It offers idiosyncratic possibility. Adaptations to change and to anticipated change flourish. Sometimes the changes are simple and lighthearted: the current fad of keeping a few hens fed organically recalls the past (however nostalgic) while evidencing a bit of control over personal diet. Chemical-free lawns reduce parental worry about toddlers and children, and larger vegetable gardens prove stunningly productive. Sometimes the changes disturb city people. The drilled well producing pure, unadulterated water, the deeper geothermal well enabling on-site heating and cooling, the solar panels on the house and garage roof generating electricity, even the new wood or pellet stove and the wood pile behind the garage whisper of family-scale planetary action, a sort of separate peace. Basement shelves lined with freeze-dried and canned food speak slightly more loudly of preparation, whispering through the centuries of grain in the byre and potatoes in the cellar. Bureaucrats yammer about miles-per-gallon mandates but remain silent about suburban houses with R-150 insulated attics, houses that cost less to heat than apartments and condos with a third the footprint. Urban planners view askance the start-up businesses thriving in spare bedrooms and basements. City people, particularly educated ones determined to bring organized salvation to suburban, rural, and small-town people, distrust such innovative adaptation if they do not fear it. They should be wary. American English offers little assurance that cities prove permanent. **Citizen** means something else, and **urbanite** connotes something scruffy and scrounging. City dwellers know they dwell, live impermanently in cityscape, that cityscape is something unnatural and perhaps unsustainable, unenduring.

The Black Death, the bubonic/pneumonic plague, the rat- and flea-borne calamity which killed two-thirds of Europe's population between 1346 and 1353, swept out of

Asia along the Silk Road into Crimea. Ships brought fleeing
Genoese merchants and infested black rats to Sicily, Genoa,
and Marseilles. From there ships took the plague to Spain
and Portugal and then to England, then across the North
Sea to what is now the Netherlands, Belgium, and Germany.
It crossed the Baltic to Scandinavia and reached Russia by
land. Huge swarms of rats migrating from famine-stricken
areas carried it everywhere. It struck especially hard in Italian cities (Venice lost two-thirds of its people and Bologna
four-fifths); city dwellers fled into rural places, as Giovanni
Boccaccio recounts in his 1353 *Decameron* set outside Florence.[5] In the northwestern part of the former Roman
Empire the plague proved appallingly lethal, killing between
a half and two-thirds of the people of England and the low-
lying lands to the east. There—especially in England—
people lacked the slight resistance of some coastal
Mediterranean people. Too many stresses pulled against
each other. The corruption of the church, the decay of feudalism in the midst of near-constant local warfare, and the
awkward incapacities of market-town and urban governance
clashed with monarchial visions of good order across large
regions. Consciously or not, monarchs, noblemen, and merchants struggled to marshal all farmers against repetitive
famine. Without good harvests little else might happen, not
even war. And harvests had become chancy.

Late in the thirteenth century began what climatologists
now call "the little ice age," the two centuries of deepening
cold and fierce storms that succeeded a long period of grad-
ual warming, the "medieval warming period" when the
European population burgeoned. In the warm centuries the

Norse settled present-day Iceland, then the east and west coasts of Greenland, and eventually pushed further to present-day Newfoundland. Sagas record Greenland coastal waters free of ice in summer, birches and other trees growing in protected spots along its shores, and plenty of grass for cattle. Around 1300 the climate changed. Suddenly. The sharp change produced the Great Famine in the British Isles and Europe. Starting with a poor spring in 1315, successive crops failed through 1317 and remained poor for another five summers. The Great Famine killed millions, produced civil disorder, led to infanticide and cannibalism, and weakened the entire population in advance of the Black Plague.

The Black Death came as unholy terror incomparably worse than famine. After its first slaying it remained endemic: it broke out again in 1361, 1371, and 1382. Some resistance developed: in 1348 almost everyone afflicted died, but by 1382 only about a fifth of Europe's population got sick and almost no one died.[6] But the staggering death toll of the first onslaught meant near-instantaneous depopulation, the specter of dead farms and hamlets and villages, whole stretches of countryside bereft of people, survivors abandoning many places and struggling to find any places of safety.[7]

In England and across northwestern Europe, the forest returned. Grass grew in city streets, something that so horrified urban survivors it shaped an enduring curse: "May grass grow in your streets." Weeds sprouted in abandoned fields, which reverted to scrub and then to woods. Roofs, thatched roofs especially, fell in, then walls collapsed. Everywhere paths vanished, and sometimes overgrown roads, blocked by fallen trees or cut by washed-out bridges, devolved into footpaths or disappeared entirely. Civil order deteriorated. Squatters and brigands used abandoned land as the base for raids and sometimes threatened fragmented military force itself. In German lingers an old word, **ortsbewüstung**, designating the bewildering or wildering of a once-maintained, ordered, loved place.[8] In English, **bewilderment** is a new term, traceable to about 1620. From its beginning it connoted being lost or confounded in a pathless place, often a dark woods, but also being confused, from the Old English **wilder**, to be led astray, as a hunter following a beast can be led astray, made lost. The English word lacks the spatial emphasis of the German. It lacks too the gritty, raw, unnerving violence of German folktales, especially those collected by Wilhelm and Jacob Grimm early in the nineteenth century.[9] The unexpurgated, translated editions of their work (Victorians made the tales suitable for children in part by excising many of the tales completely, in part by changing entire meanings—even now undergraduates must be told why the wolf lurks in bed) hammer home the appalling, powerful disorder of abandoned, grown-over, pathless places, the witch house in the middle of woods, the path luring its followers, the solitary serial killer now and then leaving his crumbling cottage in search of a young girl, the salted fingers kept as trophies. Black Death survivors, few and weak and exhausted by farm work, understood that faltering might precipitate new famine, that the trees hid the brigands come to burgle, to steal harvests and women, to kill.[10] At all costs survivors had to push back against the trees, keep the pastures and meadows and arable fields open to the sun.[11]

And the dikes collapsed. Again. For some two thousand years Frisians had been building dikes, channeling rivers, and cutting down trees.[12] The low-lying North Sea lands originally supported dense forest. **Holland**, the name for a region around present-day Dordrecht, indeed derives its name from **holt land**, **woodland**. Not so much marsh as dark swamp, the low-lying forest proved brutally hard to shape into agricultural land. For many centuries, Frisian pioneers raised mounds constructed of clay, cow manure, reeds, and water plants, some almost fifty feet above ordinary water level, as refuges from intermittent flooding. In Old Frisian **terp** designates a village, and many terps each supported fifty or even more houses and a church, along with enough land to crowd in cattle during great floods. But most terps raised only a house and farmstead buildings surrounded by low fields. In ordinary floods terps became islands on which farmers waited for high water to drain into gutters leading to tidewater.

In 1282 a great storm destroyed many of the outermost dikes and canals.[13] Five years later an immense one destroyed all, permanently overwhelming a vast area Frisians finally called the Zuider Zee, the South Sea, the name memorializing the cultural power of North Frisians suddenly staring south and inland, away from their North Sea. The 1287 Saint Lucia's Day storm, a combination of abnormally high tides and perhaps what is today called a five-hundred-year autumn cyclone, drowned between fifty and eighty thousand people overnight as it washed away countless terps. Nineteen hundred square miles vanished under fifteen feet of tidal water.[14] The new inlet inundated diked pasture,

meadow, and cropland with salt water, ended road transportation, slammed survivors into long-term hunger and
despair, and stymied flood control, navigation, and land
improvement for six centuries.[15] In 1348 the Black Death
hit a battered, weary, reduced population of survivors
stunned by the massive, permanent invasion by the sea,
struggling to repair and maintain dikes, windmills, and
canals at the edges, and frightened of another storm in an
era grown stormy. Bereft of half its population at least, the
marge adjacent to the new sea slowly flooded as built
defenses crumbled.

Not enough people remained to dike, pump, shovel up.
Century after century witnessed only incremental progress
in land making (and landscape making). His posthumously
published, six-volume *Vaderlandsche geographie* (1791)
records the lifetime effort of Willem Albert Bachiene
(1712–1783) to document the effort.[16] But not until the
1950s did the Dutch gain control of the Zuider Zee.

The St. Lucia's Day storm also inundated Dunwich in
England. The day before, the city rivaled London in population and commercial supremacy.[17] Surf damage, catastrophic
flooding, and sandbar movement began the demise at which
English folktale still shudders. (Fewer remember how the
storm also plowed into rural Norfolk, into the wetland
region called The Broads.)[18] Not all suffered: over time the
Zuider Zee made the fortune of one terp protected by a far
inland dike which held, as Amsterdam became an ocean
port and prospered. Westward stretched the new sea bordered on **ortsbewüstung**.

Willem Albert Bachiene understood the immense difficulty implicit in fusing the reclamation of land for settlement and agriculture with the need to facilitate ocean trade: here he depicts the complexity of harbor openings. Harvard College Library.

Inland from the sea but still in tidal waters, vessels are docked at wharves built at the intersection of bridges, raised roads, and the dams which gave their name to so many Netherlands towns. Harvard College Library.

Dikes and canals combined to produce and defend reclaimed land, but also to provide access, especially to animals grazing near slightly elevated villages, themselves protected by wind-driven pumps. Harvard College Library.

Pilings defended new-made land from adjacent high tides and waves: here Bachiene illustrates the continual marching seaward of made land and the usefulness of elevated ways paralleling possible flooding. Harvard College Library.

Vaderlandsche geographie emphasizes its author's understanding of landscape as worthy of sustained study and respect—and insists that what people had made from swamp, marsh, sandbars, and mud and kept safe from the sea had a distinct beauty even foreigners recognized. Harvard College Library.

For centuries thoughtful observers wondered at the Zuider Zee and its environs, and at vanished Dunwich, especially those sailing over either. They cringed at the devastation left by the 1717 coastal flood striking deep into northeast Germany, a storm which killed at least eight thousand.[19] In his 1825 poem "A Wraith in the Sea," Heinrich Heine mused about lying over the gunwale of a boat and seeing below "a city, sharp as the light of day, / medieval, netherlandish, / and teeming with life."[20] A great storm—and the Black Death—had produced something scarring, the return of wilderness, the incursion of the sea, the return of the forest, the return of the chaos that destroys what people build and maintain, that ruins stability, ruins the stead.

Stead derives from old Germanic and ultimately Indo-European roots, its cognates reaching to Sanskrit **sthiti**, meaning standing, holding position, the truly ancient root of **stationary** and **station**. In Old English and Old Frisian it designated (roughly) what today **place** denotes, but West Frisians pronounced it **stêd** while North Frisians pronounced it **städ**, perhaps (lexicographers are not sure) approximating the Old Scandinavian **stad**. The Old English **stede** evolved into something Americans use too glibly, **place** as in **homeplace** (common in the Deep South but moving rapidly into the High Plains) and "my place," as in "come over to my place" or "my place on the lake." In North Frisian, early pronunciation marks a different course, one paralleling (or helping to produce) the modern Dutch **stad** and German **stadt**, designating **town** or, in Germany, more frequently **city**. The distinction offers glimmerings of

English thinking expressed in **homestead** and **farmstead**—
intimately familiar, always reassuring words about homes
outside of cities and towns, in open-country neighborhoods,
in the shire of J. R. R. Tolkien's *The Hobbit*.[21]

The English words connote stable, long-term, family-
scale agricultural effort centered on the house and its outbuildings, not village or town business. Farmers can live in
hamlets, villages, and other nodes, but as Peter Laslett
emphasizes in *The World We Have Lost: England Before the
Industrial Age*, "before the coming of the bicycle and the
paved highway, there was a fixed distance" from the home
of the village-based farmer or agricultural laborer "beyond
which a full day's work was out of the question—it took too
long to get there and back."[22] Given civil order and certainty
(whatever the specific character of the leviathan providing
such), families found living in the center of their fields more
efficient. Livestock often requires round-the-clock attention,
and reaping field crops often proceeds under harvest moons.
Until the invention of the bicycle and other machinery,
stern rules shaped farming, the ordering of farm families,
and the arrangement of agricultural landscape.[23] For centuries families clustered in hamlets and men walked out to
fields, often driving livestock to pasture, but as population
grew, either groups hived off to start new hamlets on the
edge of forest land or—in times of peace and order—families moved out independently. The farmstead—in the
United States more often **homestead**—rooted the family in
place. In drought and in good years the family tended its
land, much of its work happening in house, barn, stable,
and other structures clustered at the center of fields, the

cluster itself more or less fenced (sometimes to catch the sun or break the wind) as a yard, but much of it happening in fields reaching in all directions from the cluster of structure. Families often cooperated, of course. Men combined horses and effort in spring plowing, women helped each other reap or put up food in autumn, neighbors assembled to build or repair houses and barns. But enterprise, family or neighbor, depended on order and stability, as did the steads themselves, and the need for this much effort meant not leaving the family's space for days on end. Leviathan power thus produced expansive but distinctly private agricultural spaces, each centered on a compact arrangement of structures, chief among them a house.

The Black Death reversed the colonization of English wilderness, especially the forest wilderness. In his 1957 *History on the Ground: Six Studies in Maps and Landscapes*, Maurice Beresford (1920–2005), another founder of landscape studies, urged readers intrigued by scarcely discernible rural ruins to look carefully and repeatedly. "Familiarity breeds comprehension," he wrote in a chapter entitled "A Journey among Deserted Villages." "As with so many archaeological features, a succession of visits leaves behind it a more comprehensive picture." Three years earlier his massive *Lost Villages of England* had analyzed not just the creation of the medieval countryside but its sudden ebb into abandonment, what Beresford emphasized in *History on the Ground*, a book aimed at determined, thoughtful inquirers exploring rural places. "What is certain is that the Black Death of 1349 and the successive returns of the plague over the next twenty years created an economic situation which was in many respects the very opposite of that which had nourished the growth of villages and the extensions of their fields," he asserted.[24] Entire village populations died, order decayed, and even the market for surplus agricultural produce collapsed. Instability clawed its way from the far edges of fields and from the forests filled with outlaws to farmsteads and shriveled villages and towns. Astute walkers might find subtle evidence everywhere in rural England. All they need do is look.

Since the early 1960s climatologists have probed what Danish, Greenland, and Canadian hikers discern: the subarctic tree line has moved south more than a hundred miles over the past four centuries. The speed of the change vexes scientists and helps explain more than the extinction of the many Norse settlements in Greenland.[25] Cold and storms from the end of the twelfth century to the middle of the sixteenth (or the early seventeenth, according to some scientists) slowed agricultural reclamation following the Black Death. Afforestation accelerated as survivors, often weakened by poor harvests into the 1550s, focused their energies elsewhere than the edges of far-off fields. Illness, and especially infant mortality, stymied economic recovery.[26] Husbandmen struggling to keep newborn lambs alive in snowstorms, to plow only the most fertile fields, and to gather ever-increasing amounts of firewood turned away from places so long abandoned they seemed unrecognizable, their mute testimony to failure engendering only despair.

In remote, rural places, landscape evidence and longstanding, quasi-folk memory combine to recall the little ice age.[27] Norse pioneers prospering in hundreds of places along the east and west coasts of Greenland found themselves cut off from Iceland and mainland Europe: ice and gales ended trade, and cut even the westward route to Vinland for building timber. From the far north came the **skraelings**, invaders clad in furs, expert hunters, people experienced in arctic conditions: over a few decades they slaughtered the rickets-stricken Norse settlers scarcely able to farm. Not until the early twentieth century did Danish scientists explore what whalers and other mariners reported anecdotally after about 1750: ruins marked the shores of most Greenland inlets inhabited by Eskimos, confirming what the final Icelandic sagas recount, the collision of settlers with people they condemned as savage.

If Columbus indeed visited Iceland in 1477 to hear firsthand the oral accounts of land in the west, what he learned of skraelings from seafarers may well explain how he treated the inhabitants of the Caribbean.[28] Against any people however remotely like those who had slaughtered Vikings living in established settlements, he moved with ruthlessness born in fear. The little ice age may well have shaped much of modern western culture. Wilderness threatened fourteenth- and fifteenth-century people, including elites. It meant more than deep sea or mountain ridges or dense forest: it meant the reach of such, ocean incursion, the advance of glaciers, blizzards blocking mountain passes for months, the afforestation of farmland, lawlessness charging from woods and marshes, famine, plague, and continuous uncertainty. It meant cold, travail, and intermittent despair. It meant instability, disorder, intermittent chaos.[29]

So the stead gathered stunning evocative power. It announced order, the order basic in the English common law which identified the yeomen of England as landowners responsible for land, for feeding the realm, for their families and farmhands, for serving on juries, inquests, and every posse a sheriff or magistrate raised, for paying taxes, for bringing their longbows to war, for obeying the law, for honoring the king. Each stead exemplified order, reinforced order, announced order. Each stead supported order too.

Against it stood the forest and marsh and often uncontrollable water, the river likely to flood, the sea likely to reach inland, and wild animals, wolves, bears, lynxes likely to kill livestock, the rats anxious to devour whole harvests and suspected of carrying plague. In the forest and marshes and along the riverbanks lurked criminals likely to prey. All the forces of disorder, even the wind, threatened the stead.

Out of the plague years and the little ice age emerged a bitter distrust of dense forest and a near beatification of the stead expressed in a deep, inchoate love of sunlit fields abutting other sunlit fields. In much folklore, especially in tales beginning "Long ago, in the reign of the good King John," the landscape of steads surrounded by fields and punctuated here and there by a castle and small villages epitomized peace, order, and plenty. That vision English colonists brought to the heavily forested new world. It shaped most of the colonization effort, even the frantic love of the log cabin surrounded by stump-filled cornfields, the homestead evolving year by year from primeval wilderness.[30] In spatial terms at least, the American dream originates in a previous public health and climatic catastrophe in which natural systems almost overwhelmed human order.

The suburban homeowner digging weeds, screening squirrels from attics, and—perhaps above all—raking leaves attempts to order nature, to control it, to keep wilderness at bay. And the suburban stead, the homestead, endures as the foundation of cultural, political, and spatial order ignored by political theorists uninterested in landscape, in rapid climatic (and perhaps public health) change, and lately unmindful of the Charter of the Forest.[31] **Sustainable city** seems an oxymoron.

As it cuts into the earth, the plow point makes a furrow as the curved share overturns soil into the adjacent furrow, making a land. JRS

6 FARM

Home for Thanksgiving, home for Christmas: in illustrating **home** the greeting card industry emphasizes that the farm remains the national emblem of the United States. Urbanization and suburbanization notwithstanding, the farm endures as the chief component in what geographers call an **open-country neighborhood** and in what so many Americans know as the American dream. The large-lot suburban home is both a homestead and vestigial fields and orchards, but the large-lot suburban landscape replicates on a finer scale the great signature landscape spreading west from the thirteen colonies.[1] Elbow room—not wanting to see, let alone smell, the smoke of neighbors' chimneys—and freedom from undue surveillance form part of the rights Americans take so easily for granted. Tolerance thrives in open-country neighborhoods. So long as they mind fields and livestock, distant neighbors prove easy to get along with because they are distant, often out of sight (or nearly so) and so out of mind, not even very well known or understood, and rarely a nuisance.

Farms epitomize the myth of the self-sufficient family. Of course the myth is false. From the beginning of colonization farmers traded, southern tobacco planters and Hudson Valley poltroons trading at larger scales than most, but everyone exchanging plantation or farm produce for blacksmith work or sugar or something else from beyond the fields. In medieval times the lord of the manor collected an annual rent, the **firma**, from each tenant farming a place. The Norman word (rooted in the Latin **firmare**, meaning to fix) morphed into **firm** and then **farm**, the pronunciation shift perhaps drawn by the genuinely ancient Old English word **feorm**, lingering in Northumberland as **færm**, apparently from a Germanic root **fermâ**, meaning food and sometimes a banquet or feast.[2] Lexicographers bicker over "firma," the editors of the *Oxford English Dictionary* insisting that if English absorbed the Latin *firmare* it must have done so extremely early, because medieval English writers in Latin understood the word as designating a feast. Greeting card companies hedge their bets: their images show the fields and buildings from which food is harvested and the houses in which it is consumed.

But farms are firms. Well into the nineteenth century some British writers used **firm** for **farm**, although by then "firm" had designated business companies of two or more individuals since the mid-eighteenth century. Agreements between or among individuals required confirmation, sometimes a firm handshake, sometimes a signature, one meaning of **firm** which entered English via Spanish and Portuguese bankers. **Company** is a much older word, derived from Latin roots meaning those who break bread together, and companies tend to move around, medieval theatrical companies moving from venue to venue, trading companies moving from trade fair to trade fair, manufacturing companies moving from one industrial city to another or far offshore. In corporate contexts, **firm** is much younger and, like **stead**, emphasizes stability: fifteenth-century English writers recorded the firming of marriages, incorporation agreements no human force might put asunder, agreements lasting until death. When a firm is a farm, it is fixed indeed, grounded in a place, steadfast, forced to succeed or fail in place. Farmers may sell out, move west in covered wagons or flee the Dust Bowl in jalopies, but they leave behind farms to be farmed by other families or devoured by wilderness or real estate developers. A family-owned farm fuses home and business. That the business produces food necessary for life only further complicates the pinning down of meaning.

Children understand early what vexes bureaucrats, jurists, and scholars. Before they can read, toddlers see pictures of a horse, a cow, a pig, a sheep, a chicken, and other farm animals typically presented as cheerful inhabitants of a happy farm. Parents read aloud names and imitate the neighing of one animal, the baaing of another, and as they do the children repeat the sounds, the turning pages presenting an idealized, appallingly dated image of a freestanding, mixed-agriculture farm prospering in rolling countryside, its neighbors simply out of the picture. Lisa Bonforte's *Who Lives on the Farm?* and countless similar books, read and reread aloud in snug, loving proximity to beloved adults, must work as one of the greatest forces shaping perception of landscape and skewing subsequent understanding of agricultural enterprise.[3] Parallel books centered on strip mines, oil refineries, logging operations, or machine tool manufacture seem almost beyond imagining.

Background governs illustrated farm books created for toddlers and young children. Almost always the barn is gambrel-roofed with hay thrusting from wide-open loft doorways. Sort of a stable but rarely a granary, the barn faces a farmyard framed by henhouse and farmhouse. Implicitly the tractor, almost invariably drawn from models built circa 1940, sleeps in the barn, never in a tractor shed. Paddocks scarcely exist. Horses and cows romp or rest in green pastures abutting barnyards, separation accomplished by a few lengths of post-and-rail fencing. Beyond the barn—sometimes—grow a few rows of corn, sometimes bright green, often beige, suggesting approaching harvest. At the far end of most scenes lies only more rolling green field interrupted with lone trees. Scale is not human; it is diminutive. Barns are small, henhouses tiny, stables sheltering no more than one or two horses. Missing are manure heaps, silos, plows, balers, and other implements the tractor might pull, and automobiles. Despite the plethora of books about trucks and cars, farm-focused books imply that one small tractor (lacking the vertical roll-over protection structure so striking in contemporary machinery silhouette) proves enough. Why horses live on the farm must mystify. Illustrators show no plows, not even wagons. Livestock appears as pets.

But children's books depict the world as adults want children to see it. Farm books are castles in the sunlit summer sand. Education and driving around introduce and explain tall blue silos, shiny sheet-metal feed transfer systems, combines and other self-propelled implements, robotized tractors, center-pivot irrigation sweeps a half-mile long. They make clear the proliferation of single-crop farms, the immense corn farms of southern Illinois supplying Texas feedlot cattle-fattening enterprises, the thousand-acre sunflower seed farms of North Dakota, the wheat fields of Wyoming. Classroom teaching and long-distance automobile trips might emphasize the scale of farming, neighborhoods in which each farm family lives in the center of a **section** of land, a square of 640 acres produced by the cadastral survey envisioned by Thomas Jefferson and his contemporaries as the best way of surveying and selling off the Louisiana Purchase and lands westward. The quintessential American farm, its farmstead smack in the center of hundreds if not thousands of acres of tilled land, strikes many city dwellers as it often strikes foreigners.[4] Lonely.

Teaching and thoughtful trips make clear that the rubber-tired tractor moves at speed along country roads paved for it, enabling farmers to work land separated from their home acreage by great fields owned by neighbors, that automobiles and school buses rocket along paved and gravel roads, that children ride ATVs along the edges of fields and find friends racing toward them, that children (little girls especially) still ride horseback to visit friends. Examining maps and driving mile after mile along section roads reveal the remnants of long-abandoned barns, houses, and one-room schools and display an enormity of scale that mocks urban standards. Scale alone conquers the preschool farm-book vision.

Farms long ago expanded beyond the quarter-section ones of 160 acres and the mites of forty acres each worked by a poor family and a mule, beyond even the full section farms. Few farmers talk today of "the back forty" or the "five more acres in the lower forty" of Bobbie Gentry's 1967 song "Ode to Billie Joe." Small farms exist, of course, and most thrive, fertilized by love and discipline and hope, but few resemble those in children's books. Many are gargantuan, yet oddly enough are still family farms, their owners having incorporated for inheritance-tax and insurance reasons, two or three generations of each family making a living on family land but noticeably—especially from a light aircraft—living in houses each formerly at the center of an independent family farm. Hired hands still work on farms, often living away from the farmstead itself, sometimes in mobile homes, sometimes in houses provided by agreement. Given the price of good acreage and the cost (even when financed) of secondhand tractors and other machinery, few hired hands ever come to own farms, at least large ones, unless they marry the farmers' daughters. Middle school and high school education might teach what long, leisurely family vacations teach to privileged children, that the staggering efficiency and scale of contemporary American farming enable about 3 percent of the population to feed the nation and much of the rest of the world.

But formal education ignores agriculture, and most American families lack the money or time or even the vehicles to make long road trips across (not necessarily to) great agricultural regions. After perfunctory lessons on the westward movement (all of which ignore the crops the pioneers

intended to grow), schools fail. What looking from Pullman
car windows once taught the privileged, what General
Motors introduced as a commercial jingle in 1949 ("See the
USA in Your Chevrolet"), what the National Park Service
hoped might happen, what did happen accidentally to thousands of children being driven west to Disneyland, has vanished in the face of cheap airfares. Today most American
agriculture flourishes in so-called "fly-over states," appearing
(on clear days) to the rare passenger looking down as squares
of different shades of green or yellow. The fly-over states
unnerve city people, especially at election time. So many are
"sparsely settled," but nonetheless each sends two senators to
Washington. They raise persistent, vexing questions about
proximity to local police ("When seconds count, the county
deputy is only forty minutes away," reads one bumper
sticker), gun ownership and lack of gun crime, and lately
about illegal drugs, rural gangs, illegal immigration, and
especially genetic engineering. Robotic tractors ruled by GPS
and on-board computers plant seeds that worry rare urban
travelers devoted to organic diets. What do modern farmers
sow, what livestock live in the immense metal buildings
located beyond wire fences and alarmed gates? What genetic
engineering already reshapes blurred-green regions? Adults
who cannot tell a field of sorghum from one of soybeans
keep their eyes on the road as they drive through fly-over
land. At home they snuggle with toddlers, drift into the picture book imagery of agrarian stability, security, and nostal-
gia. On the rural road, beyond comfort zones, they glare at
square miles of impeccably ordered, weed-free, homogenized
crops they cannot name and—less frequently in the past ten
years—at engineered animals, ostriches included.

Horses, cows, and sheep graze, typically in pastures but sometimes on the open range, free-ranging in the medieval tradition of livestock roaming land held in common. **Pascuage**, Norman and law French for such outdoor feeding, lingers in the common law, along with its cousins, **pascua**, defined by Henry Campbell Black in his *Law Dictionary* as "a particular meadow or pasture land set apart to feed cattle," and **pascua silva**, a wood devoted to the feeding of cattle.[5] As an Anglicized legal term, **pasturage** designates not only a piece of ground in which animals graze and a specific appurtenance of a piece of land—the right to graze animals on a different piece of ground—but hay cut from a pasture (not a meadow). "Anon a careless herd / Full of the pasture jumps along by him / And never stays to greet him," run the lines in *As You Like It*.[6] Little Boy Blue must blow his horn because a sheep grazes in a meadow and a cow is in the cornfield: both animals belong in a pasture.

Meadow comes from the Old English **mǽdwe**, itself seemingly rootless, although related to the Old Frisian **mêde** and the Old Dutch **mada**, the English term puzzling lexicographers as one perhaps based on regional inflection of vowels lacking in a seeming synonym, **mead**. The longer term seems as old as the shorter: both denote open grassland mowed for hay. But **meadow** (often written **myddoe**) sometime in the early sixteenth century often connoted a wet field, perhaps along a river, as herbalist William Turner wrote in 1568 of a plant which "groweth naturally in watery & marrish myddoes," *Althea officinalis*, the true marshmallow so common in North Sea salt marshes.[7] Norman scribes sometimes understood "meadow" as a synonym of **pré**, the root of the American **prairie** and different from **glade**: people make meadows.

In *The Making of the Pré*, French poet Francis Ponge records his forty-year effort to trace the connections between a riverside grassland and the prefix, at one point suggesting of the grassland, "perhaps it is to the big woods what the beach is to the cliff (there is something of the beach, of sand or fine gravel, in the pré)."[8] Until the seventeenth century, when it became essentially a literary (and especially a poetic) term, **glade** connoted dry greensward, what **lawn** connoted. Long before, **meadow** connoted something wet, as the modern German equivalent, **matte**, implies, or the plaited sedges or rushes once essential in plaiting mats. While perhaps of Teutonic origin, by the sixth century **matt** or **meatt**, both probably learned terms, collided with a similar-sounding Latin term to produce the French **nappe**, designating a table cloth. All of this mangled usage proves important when walking barefoot in meadows. Many are damp, the better to ensure two or three harvests of nutritious grass each summer, sun-dried into hay. Livestock trample grass, ruining the nap so necessary for scythes to cut. Abandonment means incursion by weeds, then woody shrubs, then trees— immediate, sustained assault from the adjacent forest culminating in victory, trees coming in as the tide comes in. Ponge seems right about beaches and cliffs, meadows and woods.

Legal tradition emphasizes the enduring importance of feeding animals belonging to cottagers and other poor people owning no land and renting only tiny lots. By early medieval times, the era of Magna Carta and especially the

Charter of the Forest, tradition permitted the poor to graze their few animals in commonly owned pastures. Apportioning grazing rights worked by eunomy, the assignment of goods according to rank. Noble families grazed many animals in the common pasturage, the yeomanry grazed fewer, cottagers grazed a handful, and the very poor perhaps only two or even one. Common pasture typically surrounded manors and small villages as a ring of open grassland outside an inner ring of arable fields regularly plowed but intermittently left fallow. Except in winter, every morning village cowherds and other children collected animals and drove them along fenced routes between fields planted to wheat, rye, and other crops to the common pastures. Each evening they herded them back. Tradition dictated some division of common pasture: little girls drove flocks of geese to small pastures reserved for them, bulls and rams often lived at length in pastures fenced strongly enough to keep them from indiscriminately breeding with cows and sheep, and horses sometimes grazed away from cattle. As legal definition suggests, cattle proved critically important, for most families more so than horses: milk (and butter and cheese) mattered, as did meat, and the power of oxen. But every manor and every village needed oxen or draft horses to plow the common arable, so families too poor to keep a horse or a team nonetheless valued draft animals.[9]

Widespread variation characterized common grazing, but a core facet involved the collection and dispersal of livestock in the village. From late spring to late autumn individual families drove or led their animals to a central spot where one or more herders took them to pasture: to the same spot herders returned them, where individuals, typi-cally young children, brought them to stables. The open area came to be called a **green** (perhaps because manure fer-tilized it well) and in the late eighteenth century sometimes a **common**: the latter usage obscures the complexity of common or open-field agriculture, especially as it existed in medieval times. Raising livestock and planting and harvest-ing field crops fused family-based work with communal effort in ways that varied across regions, nation-states, and even from village to village. Today nearly lost in schoolroom emphasis on serfs, feudalism, manors, and other lessons on the so-called Dark Ages, its ghosts drive scenery values and tourism across much of rural Europe and the British Isles. Visitors know little about the forces which produced certain scenery, but they know the scenery as beautiful or at least calming.

Grazing livestock ice the cake. Light washes green meadows, cattle or sheep stand quietly in middle-distance pasture, and nearby a pub or inn beckons with a good lunch. Tourists knowing nothing of common-field agriculture pro-nounce the views satisfying.

What they see are dim outlines of the age following the manors, the noble-and-serfs household surrounded by fields bordered by forest. **Manor** meant originally a great tract of land given by the king to a nobleman, who in turn kept part of it for his own use (locating rent-paying tenants on it) and assigned other parts forever to his chief followers, most of whom worked their holdings with tenants themselves. Lowly followers who proved themselves brave in battle might inherit tiny freeholds of their own, but typically landownership proceeded eunomically, the lesser great getting to own, others getting to rent. "Manor" meant what **barony** now means, the great lands of a baron who might with his peers produce the Magna Carta and the Charter of the Forest. Barons tended to live in small castles surrounded by agricultural land worked by their own tenants. **Manor house** in time denoted the house, barns, and other outbuildings of each high-ranking loyal follower (or his descendants) to whom tenants living in homesteads paid rent in harvested crops or in work in fields. However old the system, by the early medieval era it depended on written documentation of landownership, what survives in modern law as **boc land**, an Old English word meaning land of the book.

The *Domesday Book*, compiled in 1086 by order of William the Conqueror (written in Norman Latin and filled with pre-Conquest English and Welsh land terms dutifully copied but not understood by its compilers) remains the best-known component of the documented-ownership tradition.[10] But "manor" and "manor house" eventually changed connotation, the latter coming to mean the big house of the local gentry, the gentle people whom hereditary right freed forever from physical labor. Orthography muddles the change. The contemporary phrase "to the manner born" identifying someone with an innate sense of grace or style (attributed to the nobility) should be written "to the manor born." Large, comfortable, homey, or grand houses attract tourists who see nearby quaint villages as equally attractive if more common. Modern tourism mislays common-field farming and barons both, but thrives on traditional, small-scale agricultural setting.

Plowing fields, tending crops, and especially harvest required everyone to work, sometimes even the lord and lady of the manor house. However much Bolsheviks and their successors mix Russian serfs and English yeoman for the sake of ideology, they are right about the cooperative effort involved in producing field crops.

But they and most others tend to ignore the brutal reality of the commune. About four-fifths of the harvest went to feed livestock, especially the oxen and horses needed for plowing. Whatever rights animals had in statute law, they had more in natural law. The pasture grass and meadow hay, and a portion of the oats or wheat too, went to feed the four-footed members of the cooperative.

A nobleman's oxen or horses joined with the draft animals of the more wealthy commoners to plow land cleared from forest. Plowing proved brutal. Wooden plowshares tipped with iron exhausted animals and plowmen (thus the British plowman's lunch still offered in pubs), especially in wet springs and in heavy soil.[11] Plows broke and turned the earth as they moved forward, the plowshare folding over the sod raised by the plow point. The narrow trench cut by the point is a **furrow**.

Looking at a modern tractor fitted with an integral plow reveals something critical about essential landscape.

Furrow derives from deep roots. Down in the hole lexicographers dig still, teasing out the parts of old Germanic, anxious for a bit of light, slopping around in water. One tap root runs back to **fore** (or **vore**) designating south, but the more important evident root in Old English, **furh** (compare Old Norse **for** and Middle Dutch **vōre**), designates a trench or drain. Root meanings prove critical here, because every furrow owns a partner. Every furrow owns a land.

Flowing upward from the plow point and rolling over the plowshare as a wave strikes a beach rises what ends up upside-down alongside the furrow as a ridge of thrown-up soil, the **land**.

Plowmen throw the lands uphill to inhibit erosion. On the best fields, ones gently sloping toward the south (easily warmed and ordinarily well drained in spring and in heavy rains), plowmen start at the top, plowing a furrow along the side of the hill. The trench parallels the sun. The first land flows from the plowshare onto undisturbed land. If the ground is wet, the thrown-up land faces for a short while a trench slightly wet. On his next pass, plowing in the opposite direction, the plowman makes a parallel furrow, its land filling the adjacent one. Back and forth, slowly as the oxen or horses move the heavy, cumbersome plow, the plowman walks, struggling to keep the plow upright and moving straight.

Fields varied in size, but plowing very early produced units of measure, the furlong and the acre. **Furlong** derives from common-field plowing: it means the length of a furrow in a common field, such fields traditionally considered ten acres in area (the consideration varied by region across England). A furlong meant forty rods or poles, a linear measurement of one side of a perfect square which produced ten acres of area. Like other ancient measures, the furlong is part of a rich history: at least since the ninth century, Englishmen have equated it with the Roman **stadium**, a statute eighth of the Roman mile. At present, "furlong" denotes

220 yards, an eighth of a legal mile and one side of a square containing ten acres. **Acre**, from the Old English **æcer** and with cognates in Old Norse **akr**, Old Frisian **ekker**, and as far back as Sanskirt **ajras**, denotes a plain, open country, forest, untenanted land, but well before 1000 in England it meant a piece of plowed land. Traditionally held to be as much land as a yoke of oxen and one plowman might turn up in a day, successive English laws codified it as forty poles long by four poles broad—more generally 4,840 square yards, Parliament acknowledging that acres came in all shapes. Only in the term for a graveyard or churchyard, "God's acre," does an older, wilder sense endure in English.

"Acre" became a measurement of work applied to earth, then a measurement of earth surface, part of an intricate, sensible system of measurement. A square mile comprises 640 acres, for example, just as a furlong totals forty rods of sixteen and a half feet each, each rod one quarter of the surveyor's chain. French revolutionaries and other metric-system advocates ignore a fundamental facet in traditional British measures. The measures emphasized division of wholes, especially among the poor. What is sold by the dozen divides easily among groups of one, two, three, four, and six people, if not among five or ten. Understanding that days consist of two dozen hours but that light and dark vary by seasons often escapes children learning about feudalism: plowing is a spring and autumn enterprise, something done in days shorter than summer.

Teenagers miss geometric significance. A square field is not a rectangular one. A square four feet on a side comprises sixteen square feet. So does a rectangle two feet by eight feet.

But the rectangle has a perimeter not of sixteen feet but of twenty. A rectangular field requires far more effort and material to fence, and the longer fence requires more effort to maintain. Farmers have known this since time immemorial, and so square fields endure wherever crops need to be protected from wandering animals.

Crop rotation meant that some common fields might be fallow in one year, that plowmen might be turning over the sod in a pasture so it might be planted to wheat, that a meadow might be used as pasture, and so on. Fences enclosed most fields, and most farmers prized square fields generally adapted to rotating needs. Fences either enclosed livestock or fenced them out, since livestock might be in any field sooner or later. Driving livestock from farmsteads or villages to and from fields required narrow ways fenced on both sides so that animals did not wander into crops. Ways were just that, **ways**. If they dead-ended at the outmost field, locals knew them as **lanes**. Passable for carts and wagons, especially at harvest, most were one rod wide, just wide enough for two wagons to pass each other. Neither roads nor highways, ways and lanes organized access to the complex field system in which everyone worked, even the elderly women caring for babies and toddlers while young mothers followed men with scythes, even the old men caring for hens and other small stock never driven out to pasture. Expressions like **cart path** endure in rural American speech, especially in the former colonies, correctly designating narrow ways (in New England often lined with stone walls now overwhelmed by forest) used by farmers. **Cow path** misleads. Cow paths are not narrow, twisting paths slightly larger than footpaths: cows amble along in groups, like being side by side, and so make wider paths, most of them long ago abandoned or eventually used as public ways, as roads. But ways and lanes and stone walls variegate the fields tourists admire, city dwellers vaguely imagine, and little children see simplified in picture books.

Over centuries the common-field system in Britain evolved into one emphasizing the freestanding farms of yeoman families and the smaller ones leased by tenants of the gentry residing in manor houses often not much larger than those owned by prosperous freeholders. Rural economic change sometimes moved at near-glacial speed, sometimes like lightning (as in the eighteenth-century Enclosure Period when many poor people lost their rights to common grazing and Parliament divided the last common fields into individual holdings), but it happened still, even in the most traditional of places. Population growth drove it. Existing fields and new fields laboriously clawed from forest eventually could not accommodate the rising generation of young people, some of whom moved on, sometimes to sea or to new colonies, or shifted into industry, or struggled, erecting cottages in what struck them as no-man's land, maybe the king's forest. Fields too far from a village, too far to walk to and return, meant a hiving off, and so long as the king maintained order, families slipped away from villages to live on freestanding farms.

Royal power, leviathan itself in Hobbesian thinking, joined divine in ordering official movement onto land and the conveyancing of land from one party to another. The king and his knights, sheriffs, coroners, and other officials guaranteed peace, the orderly conveyancing of land (especially title) described in **metes and bounds**: so many paces from the great oak, down to the four rocks in the brook, east to the royal highway, all the never-lost language of land description recorded in castles and county courthouses. In Holy Scripture everyone read the dictate of Proverbs 22:28, "Remove not the landmark." On All Hallows Eve peasants carved large turnips into effigies of Jack o' the Lantern, the spirit known to steal or move boundary markers: long before Britain became a Roman province and learned to worship Terminus, god of boundaries, it knew Jack and the nasty confusion following landmark destruction.[12] Today few intellectuals think of the county courthouse as a library, but its archive of recorded deeds and wills, the last decentralized records in the United States, maintain civil and spatial order by preserving title to steads and fields. Just as sandcastles mark the fragmentation of family realm on any beach, so castles guarantee still the permanence of landownership and the rights to enjoy and bequeath improvements. They maintain too—if only in ordinary county courthouses—the words so critical in knowing landscape intimately, firsthand, the words of built spatial order mirroring political order.

Language, especially legal language, hints at the colonization of difficult places throughout the British Isles, and "furrow" illuminates something crucial in any understanding of essential landscape.

In deeds, "land" often denotes each strip of plowed land in a large damp field cut by **water furrows**, a strip being roughly eighteen feet wide. Away from marshy rural areas, "furrow" no longer connotes a drain open to the sun (unlike

gutter, which denotes a secret passage of water, or at least one obscured by reeds if not built covering), but **water furrow** does. Deciphering significance involves knowing **grip**, a word now obsolete (at least in polite language) except among hunters, rooted in the Old English **grép** somehow altered by the Middle Dutch **greppe** (which became the more modern **groop**) in parts of English once pronouncing **sheep** as **sip**.[13] A "gryppe, or a gryppel, where water rennythe a-way in a londe, or water forowe," in the words of one writer in 1470, Anglicus Galfridus, distinguishes between dry land, perhaps raised, and submerged land, in a made trench.[14] The submerged-land meaning appears to have disappeared by 1500, with "land" meaning what farmers know as dry land, including land raised from wet. Unlike a ditch dug with a shovel, a water furrow is plowed, and on one or both sides raises a strip of soil, a land: a digger may toss the soil broadly on adjacent soil, but the plowman cannot. Water furrows happen when a plowman reverses direction one furrow away from plowed land and throws the land opposite the adjacent furrow, not into it: not until 1665 did a surveyor, George Atwell, suggest that water furrows be dug with a spade.[15] Between Galfridus and Atwell **landscape** entered English as the term for made land, land plowed or shoveled up from wet land, especially the wet land along the North Sea coast so inimical to farming that local squires sent to the Netherlands for experts in drainage and landschop. In Lincolnshire, especially in the third of the county still called "Holland" by locals, foreigners plowed up language too, often in describing land made for meadows.

Nineteenth-century luminist painters Martin Johnson Heade and Fitz Hugh Lane prized New England salt marshes as especially rich subjects. Listening to museum visitors seeing their paintings for the first time means now and then hearing them struggle to designate marshes dotted with haystacks set atop staddles to preserve drying hay from high tides. What farmers still call **salt meadows** visitors hesitantly designate **water meadows**. Somewhere in their memory pulses the notion that meadows might be damp but can be wet indeed.

In the seeming traditional but always ever so slightly evolving rural landscape, especially that of England, perhaps New England, certainly in picture books aimed at the very young, flourish the deepest of values, understandings of peace and plenty (or at least enough for everyone in famines) and order, and of aesthetics too. In all urban parks, arborists prune trees at a height farmers call the **browse line**, dictated by the longest stretch of a hungry cow or horse, the browsing making uniform open space beneath the crown of every tree. Underlying such values—including visual ones—gently pulses a core understanding passed from one urban generation to the next: in spring farmers must plow so they may harvest in fall. In the depths of World War I Thomas Hardy caught the idea in his poem "In Time of 'The Breaking of Nations,'" noting

> a man harrowing clods
> In a slow silent walk
> With an old horse that stumbles and nods
> Half asleep as they stalk

and concludes, "this will go onward the same / Though Dynasties pass."[16] Farmers must farm and fields remain fields.

Landscape is not cityscape. Whatever their attributes, cities cannot feed themselves. Cut transportation from rural places and cities starve. So terrible is such a prospect that children inured to televised violence rarely encounter it directly. Instead they learn of farms and farmers long before they go to school. The illustrated books forge a core understanding of agricultural landscape *and* a certainty that farms and farmers will feed everyone always. Harvest, plenty, however defined, having enough to eat all the time is one driving force in knowing essential landscape.

A 1764 arched bridge endangers navigation, braces itself against flood and moving ice, and demonstrates how little pedestrians know of who or what might lurk at the opposite end of the river crossing. JRS

7 WAYS

Toddlers learn about bridges, but not by toddling along. Adults read aloud the tale of three billy goats anxious to cross a bridge leading to rich pasture. Under the bridge lives a troll which snacks on passers-above.[1] However young children understand the gentle farm herbivores (billy goats included) and pastures and meadows of preschool farm picture books, a surprising number enter kindergarten knowing that he-goats butt.[2] Many young children approach narrow footbridges warily.[3] Trolls might not exist. But under bridges anything might lurk, reach up, snatch, drown, munch. Built to make crossing brooks and rivers convenient, bridges nonetheless threaten.

Lonely bridges prove perfect for robbers. Arched bridges work especially well. The solitary wayfarer, perhaps a red-hooded damsel hurrying homeward at nightfall, cannot see the villain crouching on the far side of the arch. Railings or parapets, even the water below, make sideways avoidance difficult. The victim must fight or turn around and flee.

Paired robbers can lurk under the ends of bridges and leap out when their victim reaches the middle: scrambling up from each end, they make the bridge a trap.

Bridges offer right-angle opportunity, of course. One can throw something off the Tallahatchie Bridge. Or any bridge. One can throw oneself off the Tallahatchie Bridge, as Bobbie Gentry sang in "Ode to Billie Joe."[4] Bridges reward sustained scrutiny, especially when one walks midway, stops, and looks around.

Any thoughtful walker realizes that bridges control. Their placement channels traffic to specific crossing points. Design and construction often constrict waterborne trade or else inhibit road traffic. Bridge piers intensify currents and make navigation perilous: low decks stop most vessels. Drawbridges facilitate the passage of vessels but impede pedestrian and vehicle movement. Arched bridges, for centuries the strongest sort of compromise, permit small vessels to pass under and heavy loads to pass over but nonetheless force people and draft animals to exert themselves. The bail of the pail might be the same length whether up or flat along the rim, but going around a river is usually not an option: going around a hill is easily accomplished, but people and animals must force themselves over arched bridges. Today, especially in cities, motorists scarcely notice the arched bridges which replaced the obsolescent movable bridges once essential to long-gone sailing-ship traffic. A gentle press of the accelerator pedal slides the automobile up and over new bridges arched just enough to accommodate pleasure boats. But the new bridges distort pedestrian traffic. People will walk blocks out of their way to stay on level ground, preferring not-yet-replaced flat movable bridges to new arched ones. In coastal and lake- and riverfront cities, arched bridges defy all urban design effort aimed at encouraging walking and bicycling. An arched bridge remains what it has always been, half convenience, half impediment, but nowadays seen mostly from land, rarely from water: when seen from the air, an arched bridge strikes many observers as flat.

Bridges blossom at the headwaters of ocean navigation, where estuaries and bays become too shallow for oceangoing ships. At headwaters ships anchor or dock to transfer cargo: often they transfer some freight to barges operating further inland. Transshipment foci become hubs of land trade, goods moving from shore to ship as well as from ship to shore. Ferries first link the busy sides of the estuary, dodging lighters and small boats and deep-sea vessels. As cross traffic grows, ferries prove cumbersome and expensive: eventually some leviathan, the king or his subordinates, sometimes a proto-local government, commissions a bridge.

London exists by reason of location and prospers by improvement. Ribbons of natural high, hard ground converged at a narrow point, making good places for ships to land cargo on shore and a low-tide ford across the Thames. The first bridge at the transshipment point, probably a floating pontoon bridge (with a movable part to allow river vessels to meet oceangoing ones) built by the Romans, focused road traffic: by AD 55 a garrison guarded a timber pile bridge.[5] After the legions left Britain, the Thames separated the warring kingdoms of Wessex and Mercia, the bridge disappeared (perhaps through lack of maintenance), and not until about 990 did another wood one supplant it. The stone arch bridge of the nursery rhyme begun in 1176 and completed in 1209 strained the royal treasury: eventually kings leased building lots atop it, which in time supported some two hundred houses and warehouses (some seven stories tall). Construction strained the arches. Now and then one buckled or collapsed, prompting the nursery rhyme.[6] Newcomers marveled at the bridge, its towering structures, and its gatehouses ornamented by the spiked, tarred heads of executed traitors and other criminals. Paul Hentzner, a German attorney visiting the bridge in 1598, counted thirty of the heads while wondering at the stream of traffic across the structure.[7] The Great Fire of 1666 swept the bridge of structures and weakened the arches. The City of London replaced it with another stone arch one which again distorted tidal flow but lacked structures, and which endured until replaced in 1831. Purchased in 1968, disassembled, and reerected in Arizona by a real estate developer, that bridge was replaced by the existing structure, as usual built alongside the one slated for abandonment and demolition.

Bridges fascinate little children. At the beach they dig narrow channels and moats around sandcastles and bridge them with bits of driftwood. Once noted, the inquirer finds the behavior everywhere children play at landscape making.

Bridge has deep roots stretching sideways. Derived from the Old English **brycg**, synonymous with the Old Frisian **brigge** and Middle Dutch **brugghe**, it meant and still means among longshoremen, coastal mariners, and entrepreneurial estuarine farmers what the Old Norse **bryggja** denotes: a wharf, landing stage, movable pier, or gangway. To coastal people, a bridge first of all connects the shore or a quasi-permanent structure with the side of a ship, even with a boat. A road traveler might board a rowboat or larger vessel from the hard ground adjacent to a bridge: a farmer might transship a crop at the same point. At any road bridge a traveler might find a ditch or larger hollow dug into hard ground and filled with water, perhaps only at high tide, made to accommodate small and large vessels transshipping cargo or for repairing them. Mariners and alongshore people still know any such hollow as a **dock**, a word crucial in any understanding of essential landscape.

Of "dock" the *Oxford English Dictionary* editors note bluntly, "ulterior origin uncertain." Why the term has no known origins puzzles. It is a word new in English, found fully formed in mid-sixteenth-century writing, just after it appeared in Dutch as **docke**. In the 1909 revised edition of his 1881 *An Etymological Dictionary of the English Language*, Walter W. Skeat notes that "the history of the word is very obscure." He suggests a possible connection with a provincial English word, **doke**, meaning a hollow or depression, something like the modern German **deuk** meaning a dent, but insists that the modern Norwegian **dokk** designating a hollow seems utterly unrelated to the English term lifted from the Dutch circa 1550. Like all determined lexicographers, Skeat notes the problem posed by period translation dictionaries. Randle Cotgrave's 1611 *Dictionarie of the French and English Tongues* understands the new word as the synonym of the French **haute**, a term long supplanted by **forme** and the more modern **bassin**. The word spread fast, carried by Dutch and English mariners to harbors everywhere, but its origin in the Netherlands and instant acceptance in English confuses more than dictionary makers and inquirers into landscape.

Landsmen all too often use "dock" to designate raised built structures abutting water intermittently occupied by stopped boats. This is wrong. "Dock" names an enclosure, as in the British court system, which provides for railed enclosures in which stand the accused. **Wharf** designates the structure abutting a dock.

"Wharf" derives from the late Old English **hwearf**, akin to the Middle Low German **warf**, meaning a mole, dam, or, in the words of the *Oxford English Dictionary*, a "raised site protected from flooding." The word appears in East Frisian as **warf** and modern Dutch and German as **werf**, meaning shipyard. Until the early seventeenth century it routinely designated embankments or dams, but well before that in English it named a permanent structure of wood or stone alongside which ships lay to transship cargo. **Landing stage** properly designates a less permanent, somewhat flimsy wooden structure likely to be damaged by storms: **staging**, what carpenters erect against buildings, retains the sense of impermanency. Waterfront terminology rewards the closest possible study: once spelled **qwerf** (at least in Scotland and the north of England), "wharf" is probably kin to **key** and **quay** and **hawe**, the last meaning in Old English an enclosure, especially a churchyard, and evolving through the Scottish and northern English **heugh** into **hoe**, a word enduring now only in place names, **Plymouth Hoe** perhaps being the best known, designating a turning-in spot. **Pier**, a word which mystifies linguists, appears rarely in twelfth-century writing, disappears until the end of the fourteenth century, and becomes common only in the seventeenth. It designates either the supports of a bridge, arched or not, or a substantial (often stone), raised structure which protects ships from storms or facilitates their loading and unloading, and sometimes both. The mid-sixteenth-century usage seems to have identified structures more like bulwarks than wharves: **bulwark** only muddies the alongshore waters.

Although **hoe** was unknown in Old Norse, Skeat argues that it derived from Scandinavian origins, essentially the roots of **bole** and **work**, and means anything built of tree trunks, and somehow found its way into English, Dutch, and German. But a possible Middle High German origin lies in the concept of "throwing on the ground," what soldiers do in throwing up ramparts; this is certainly how mid-sixteenth-century English writers knew the word, although they typically meant earth thrown up to channel rivers or to defend against ocean storms. A small, floating, raftlike contrivance attached to a bulwark or mole or wharf to make easier the making fast of boats and ships is called a "bridge" in Britain. But a bridge might be only a plank laid from hard dry ground to a small boat floating a few feet away: larger vessels sometimes required gangplanks, planks ganged together, assembled. These structures have their own peculiar authorities: **wharfingers** have ruled over wharves, at least in English writing, since the middle of the sixteenth century. In law they occupy a peculiar position, masters of structures built over water.

All of this matters. A lot. Where tidal water and rivers and roads come together illuminates much of essential landscape. Bridges typically have railings or parapets: wharves

and piers do not. Contemporary parents unused to the seacoast discover the sheer drop beyond the edge of wharves and
piers as they grab young children about to tumble over cap
rails. Sometimes such parents complain that wharves and
piers should have railings. But a wharf is not a bridge for all
that it bridges land and boats and ships. It is something else,
often as much protection of a dock otherwise exposed to
wind and waves as it is a permanent construction thrown up
next to the water, and railings would impede the transshipment of fish and other cargo. Rocks and mud shoveled or
dredged to make the indentation of the dock become the
wharf (or more likely, pier), the dock being not so much an
arm of the sea as perhaps a finger, the wharf or pier being
neither terp nor landscape but cousin to both. The thrown-
up rock and mud and shells augment **hithes** (or **hythe**, as in
Hythe Bridge in Oxford, the word derived from the Old
English **hyð** and unknown in any other Germanic language),
natural landing places, **shouts** (from the Middle Dutch
schûte, a flat-bottomed boat) from which one can yell for a
wherryman whose flat-bottom rowboat touches hithes efficiently and, at the ends of bridges, most conveniently.

Where salt water, rivers, and roads intersect, typically at
the head of small and large harbors, English words float in
mist, their origins and period meanings bound up in the
making of land from the sea or marsh or mudflats. Contemporary usage hints that right there, at ebb tide or flood,
whether the river flows strongly or not, however new or old
the bridge, mid-sixteenth-century English thrives.

Just a bit inland, alongshore language sometimes
becomes either riverine or roadish, the speech of travelers

more than the language of families happy to stay on farms, to relish steads and curtilage, meadows and plowed land. **River** itself derives from the same roots that produced and nurture **riven** and **rivalry**. Both connote division and separation, trouble with fords, bridge-building expenses, slippery, placeless people, even trolls.[8] English includes many river words, among them **weir** (sharing roots with **wreath**) and **riffle**, all of which blossomed in the well-watered American colonies and regions west, but it has many more words designating roads, especially older, quasi-legal ones like **roadway** hammered together (often in the aftermath of the Norman Conquest) from older words of travail and travel.

Paths occur almost naturally. People dwelling in a place, however briefly, tend to leave footprints in the grass between their tents or other shelters. Given a bit more time and regular to-and-fro perambulation, the flattened grass becomes a path. **Path**, in Old English **pæþ** and Old Frisian **path**, is a **trace** formed incidentally by people walking more than a few times, not made expressly for travel, typically not fenced, and rarely wide enough for carts and other wheeled vehicles. "Trace" is rare now, remembered in the **Natchez Trace** of course and the repetitive meaning apparent to children tracing lines on thin paper. Its origin is Norman French, **trace**. It connotes a way which vanishes, leaving behind nothing when foot traffic ceases.

Way is far older, hoary, distant kin of Sanskrit **vah**, meaning to travel or carry, but likely not of the Latin **via**: its cousins, for example **wain** as in **hay wain**, are old too, rooted in Old English and Old Frisian. It means a **track** (a new word derived from "trace") improved for travel (typically

by felling trees, removing stumps, filling mud holes, and—
less often—digging drainage ditches on either side) and typically passable by carts and wagons, including hay wains,
something denoted in **wagon way** (and in **cart path**). Other
cousins connect it with weighing, especially being weighed
down, and with travel, travail, and work, the hard work of
digging out bogged-down carts, especially in rain. Biblical
and ecclesiastical language, "all ye who travail and are heavy
laden," for example, have shaped it over two millennia, as has
the common law, especially in complex contexts of rights of
way.[9] Since at least the early seventeenth century, the plural
form has flourished alongshore: ships slide down ways when
launching. Ways, like roads, may or may not be bridged.
Roads tend to carry riders and horses can swim rivers, sometimes. Bridges appear first on roads, then on lesser ways, then
on paths, even if made from fallen trees.

    Road derives from **ride**: the Old English **rád** and Frisian
reed are variants of the past tense of **ride**. Sir Walter Scott
forever jumbled **road** and **raid** in his 1805 "Lay of the Last
Minstrel," inventing **raid** from Scottish thin air and the Old
English root. The Old English term connotes nothing of
horseborne attack, but slips into the British tradition of
knights, sheriffs, and lesser nobility riding horseback past
farmers and foot travelers. Owning a saddle horse parallels
the right to wear a sword: both imply income from tenants
farming rented land surrounding a manor house, gentleman
status. As R. F. Delderfield emphasizes in his 1967 novel *A
Horseman Riding By*, the lord of the manor, by the eighteenth
century nicknamed **squire** (the term formerly designating
the pledged assistant of a knight), regularly rode around his

small realm. Some of the ways he took, his riding, became in time his roads, something nebulously traced in the North Riding of England and the Great North Road. Class suffuses English folksong, especially Christmas carols, in lines like "God bless the master of this house wherever he may ride," and perhaps the deep love of horses in the American colonies and the United States until about 1910, when this love morphed into one for automobiles. Politicians routinely claim that house ownership, what they call **homeownership**, exemplifies the American dream, but owning and driving a motorcar seems equally important.[10] In American mythology, anyone may ride, join the gentry, sweep out onto roads and the king's highways: getting a driver's license at age sixteen means crossing the threshold to adulthood, taking charge of the mechanical steed, being accepted as an equal by all other motorists—and ever so slightly feared by all pedestrians.[11] Of course motorcar ownership figures prominently in British class division too: however much Ratty loves messing about in rowboats, it is Toad of Toad Hall who buys a motorcar in Kenneth Grahame's 1908 *The Wind in the Willows*. Great emotion walks and gallops along roads, raising intractable issues of discrimination and definition implicit in road words.

Lane connotes a dead end, a way leading to fields, often to the field farthest from the manor house, farmhouse, or village, but often at the edge of the forest devolving into a path. Rooted in the Old English **lane** and the North Frisian **lana** and **lona**—synonyms but pronounced and spelled differently—and the sixteenth-century Dutch **laen**, the word denotes a narrow **byway** (or **bye-way**), often what mid-sixteenth-century

Englishmen called a **turnagaine** or **turnagaine lane**, meaning a dead end. It also denotes, and has since the sixteenth century, a narrow way through ice fields, a mariner's synonym for **vein**: like **road,** which seamen use to designate a harbor safe in most wind directions, and **roadstead**, a harbor safe in all types of storms, "lane" has a strong seagoing constitution which in time produced segregated **steamship lanes**, English Channel **traffic lanes**, and modern highway lanes separated by white or yellow solid and dashed lines. **Bye-way** (and **by-path** or **byepath** and **bye-lane**) connotes first narrowness and then rare use: narrowness matters to anyone driving a cart, wagon, or carriage, since oxen and horses prove notoriously awkward at backing up in confined space. It is one thing to bog down a cart in mud, but something else entirely to find a byway blocked or withered into a footpath. Being bogged down is bad but being swamped is worse. Despite effort with axe, shovel, and crowbar, the frantic, exhausted wayfarer often gets nowhere except turned around. **By the way** names something away from the main-traveled road or chief purpose, something that may distort or destroy a trip or intent. A newer spelling grown stronger, **byeway** (especially as an adjective) retains the silent vowel which often indicates a masked but powerful older meaning, as it does in the word **goodbye** (a contraction of "God be with you"). In contemporary written English lingers something of serious finality. Loved ones headed off on byeways, off the usual lanes or main-traveled roads, may not certainly return. Acknowledged or not, tradition and superstition cause many contemporary people to say **so long** or **see ya** rather than **goodbye**, especially when speaking to a loved one leaving home on an adventure, especially to grown children going to war, perhaps in the hope that the ways leading away will loop back, not dead-end.

Farewells memorialize still-deep cultural issues fused with landscape. The rural Yankee **take care** unnerves travelers walking, driving, or sailing away after getting directions. The Irish **may the road rise to meet you** connotes worries about low-lying roads, getting bogged down, even the boggy man, the bogeyman of today.

Roads at least offered the possibility of horsemen riding alongside each other, each horse walking or trotting in a rut left by a cart, and perhaps three horses abreast moving along, the center one in the trace left by lone horses pulling carts in poor areas—the origin of the expression **one-horse town**. Roads connected manor houses, villages, towns, and nascent cities, not necessarily directly but in ways that eliminated the specter of dead ends except in bad weather, when wind dropped trees or water made fords impassable. Over short distances most roads proved the best route, not always the shortest in time but usually the least in effort and the greatest in certainty, especially for strangers. Locals might take short cuts, faint paths over hills and ridges or through swamps and forests, but longer-distance travelers, especially those with wheeled vehicles, preferred roads, especially those wide enough for two wagons to pass, one pole wide, sixteen and a half feet.[12]

Long-distance travelers prized protection, and the royal highway offered it even if it failed sometimes to provide. The expression **highway robbery**, a term critical in understanding beach castles, connotes the offer of protection implicit in **highway**. From the castle radiated order fitfully kept by noblemen resident in manors who handled minor crimes and who joined sheriffs and bailiffs arrived from castles to apprehend serious criminals. Over centuries, royal mandate resulted in ways raised slightly above grade and well-enough drained to be passable in wet weather. Highways were indeed high and in time paved with crushed stone, often stone crushed by imprisoned, convicted highwaymen. But other order suffused the royal highway. Along the highway rode the king's heralds and messengers, and in time the royal mail, itself in time aboard a coach carrying a few passengers and moving in stages from inn to tavern to inn, changing horses frequently. The stagecoach might or might not pass horsemen, but even when rolling slowly demanded at least a rudely graded, rudely drained way free from bandits. Far from castles and villages and even manor houses, often at night or in the middle of forests, the royal messenger or group of merchants or, centuries later, the mail coach proved a tempting target for masterless, placeless men armed with crossbows or, in later centuries, cloaked horsemen armed with pistols.

In search of such criminals went knights and sheriffs and the posse integral to the common law, the local men familiar (more or less) with nearby forests, all inquiring at farmhouses, cottages, and inns, seeking out the pathless places hiding the wicked. Outside of folksong, little of this shapes contemporary life unless the belated walker finds old fears growing as night falls in the forest or the Interstate Highway motorist suddenly realizes the broad strips of lawn abutting the shoulder, making leaving the pavement a bit safer, lawns opening the road to the sun, banishing the threat of highwaymen leaping from dark trees crowding what highway engineers still call the **carriage way**. The Interstate Highway, built by all taxpayers but open only to motorists (not to bicyclists, drivers of farm implements, and others, a brutally frank statement of class distinction), like so many great bridges open only to motorists, proves more restricted than the medieval highway. In 1400 any peasant might walk and move aside for galloping horsemen. Today pedestrians and bicyclists remain banned from the high-speed highways everyone accepts as limited-access ways. At cloverleafs, stopped for gas and quick food, motorists find wayfarers hoping to hitch rides. **Hitchhiker** harks backs to harness, wagons, lifts, teams hitched to whiffletrees and neaps, the equipage of long-distance travel before railroads. Ways, roads, the essence of roads, highways, prove critical in any understanding of landscape; and road terminology, changing so fast in the sixteenth century but still waiting at any truck stop for the thoughtful traveler, deserves a book, perhaps one written by an experienced wayfarer.

Here ways and terms can only link and inform the first sweep of landscape into something else, **townscape** and **cityscape**, larger beads on the strings of ways, roads, and highways connecting hamlets and villages.

Contemporary speed distorts understanding of highway nodes. As Mary Chapin Carpenter sings in "I Am a Town," long-distance Interstate Highway motorists see every village and small town as "a blur from the driver's side," something disappearing in rear-view mirrors. Urban motorists embarked on coast-to-coast trips rarely ponder the design of

Interstate Highway cloverleafs, let alone try to designate them. Almost never do highway speed limits drop much as entrance and exit ramps appear: weaving lanes permit traffic to leave and merge freely, with the freedom that names **freeways**. But cloverleafs trouble amateur lexicographers. Not villages, not dwellings, they nonetheless provide motels, gas stations, and restaurants for long-distance travelers, employment for people who seem to live elsewhere, and somehow some businesses serving nearby locals. As envisioned at the end of World War II, the Eisenhower Interstate Highway System has sixteen thousand cloverleafs, which represent sixty-four thousand new places in which to start new businesses, some of which bankrupted nearby hamlet and small-town commercial activity. Whatever else a cloverleaf is, it represents a spectacular example of real estate development driven by politics and road travel. Especially in rural and wilderness areas, the "sparsely settled regions" that slightly unnerve urban and suburban travelers, every cloverleaf might be the isolated tavern or inn of European and British folktale.

Inns enabled wealthy travelers to sleep indoors after a hot supper, something important over millennia of western history. Inns—and especially the taverns renting two to six rooms on less-traveled ways—offered locals the chance to gather, especially on Saturday night, talk over local affairs, and with luck hear a stranger stopped for the night speak of places beyond the woods or hills. Inns needed business to endure let alone prosper, local custom as well as the haphazard flow of travelers along the road, the locals providing income year round, the travelers ebbing and flowing with the seasons. Inns prospered according to location, of course. One halfway between towns might do well despite having few locals living nearby: strangers struggled to reach it by day's end, anxious for hot food and bed and stabling for horses. In English literature the Admiral Benbow in which opens Robert Louis Stevenson's 1883 *Treasure Island* proves one of the most enduring, just as Blind Pew's tap-tap approach to it proves one of the most frightening evocations of the empty road reaching away from an isolated inn. In the Benbow the local squire and physician now and then rendezvous, listening to the yeomen and field hands (and so learning words few other educated people, especially urban elites, knew) and eyeing the one-legged mariner who has put up for a few weeks in a room overlooking the sea. The lonely inn remains one of the stock features of historical fiction, but lately shapes all fantasy literature more or less patterned on Tolkien's *The Lord of the Rings*, in which dangerous roads and paths, and dangerous inns, figure largely.[13]

Tolkien the philologist loved tramping half-abandoned footpaths and hearing local dialect. Perhaps he knew John Ray's 1674 *Collection of English Words Not Generally Used*, the first dialect dictionary published in England. A wide-ranging botanist and Fellow of the Royal Society, Ray never forgot his humble origins: he listened to locals as he worked, in time collecting words as well as plant specimens, and he cautioned his readers that around educated people the locals grew guarded, using standard words if they could. He knew the Welsh word "bree" designating a hill, but in the country north of London he learned the English word **bree** and its meaning: to frighten.[14]

In *The Lord of the Rings* the Prancing Pony inn sits within the town walls of Bree, a place no longer prospering at the intersection of two nearly deserted highways. Civil unrest and vague threats from far off have ruined trade, and one highway has so grown up in grass the innkeeper calls it the Greenway. Tolkien wove English folklore and medieval history into his novel along with his love of northern European philology, ancient tales outside of books, and variant writing. At Bree the hobbits and dwarves slide into the English folklore of abandonment following plague and civil disorder: the highways grow unsafe and the Black Riders roam at will among bandits and the wandering poor. The travelers hire a ranger as their guide and leave the inn and then the highway as soon as they can, following faint paths into dense marsh. No road rises to meet them. Tolkien's knowledge of English folklore orders a mass of subsequent fantasy writing, science fiction, and postapocalyptic imagining. The sequence of the 1977 film *Star Wars* in which Luke meets some remarkable creatures in a tavern derives from what Tolkien knew about ways and inns, what German scholars call **strassenromantik**, the romance of the way.[15]

In the last five chapters of the first book of *The Lord of the Rings* readers discover not only the deepening importance of place names and disused landscape terms but the terrifying power of wilderness returned.[16] Fog confuses the hobbits crossing the barrow downs, Bree withers at the crossroads of bewildered ways growing up in grass, dangerous wayfarers and a sinister-seeming ranger collect at an inn, escape means leaving the grass-grown road for paths hard to find let alone follow, the two-day crossing of treacherous marshes, then the rush to a hilltop overlooking abandoned, grown-over landscape. Travel involves following a track "that seemed chosen so as to keep as much hidden as possible from the view, both of the hilltops above as of the flats to the west." From high ground the party (and the pack pony, which displays a gift for finding paths) flees south, desperate to reach a bridge over the Greyflood called the Last Bridge. Beyond the Last Bridge the river widens and no ferries link the banks: the narrow approaches to the bridge seem perfect for ambush. "The land before them sloped away southwards, but it was wild and pathless: bushes and stunted trees grew in dense patches with wide barren spaces in between," writes Tolkien of a broad region abandoned by everything, even the birds, but filled with ruins, crossed by paths scarcely discernible, and yet somewhere abutting the lands of the Fair Folk, the elves. An academic wedded to philology and to studying standing stones and other ruins on the narrow, half-forgotten ways he hiked and in the wilder areas through which he scrambled as Halliwell did and as the hobbits must, Tolkien produced a great adventure—and a great introduction to the collision of abandonment, paths and roads and villages, and wilderness in larger linguistic frames. "*Ai na vedui Dúnadan! Mae govannen!*" shouts the noble who rides up to them astride a white horse, his greeting announcing the promise of elven help and—among educated readers, even the young—something of the white horse integral to so much British folklore of bewilderment, danger, and wilderness.[17]

Tolkien shaped subsequent fantasy writing, and especially that aimed at bright children reading well above age levels.[18] He shaped too dystopian fiction, especially that centered on climate disruption or nuclear holocaust: much of *The Lord of the Rings* centers on landscape poisoned by evil, industrial processes that skew weather, light, and color.[19] His precise, extended description of landscape and wilderness inside larger cultural contexts, especially that of the dangerous, essentially abandoned road, the broken road of so much British and American folklore, shapes many settings in film, television, and especially computer games. Alan Lee emphasizes the power of Tolkien's description in the making of the film versions of *The Hobbit* and *The Lord of the Rings*. "I love stories of the wildwood, and the way our reading of it affects, and is affected by, our own experience of woods, especially those we recall from childhood, when trees really were giants," he writes in a monograph about creating the film set of *The Lord of the Rings*. "In England old woods survive if they are on marginal land, too rocky or waterlogged for cultivation." *The Lord of the Rings Sketchbook* emphasizes emotional and visual marginality: "This uneven ground, with its hollows and banks where roots become exposed, with fallen trees that continue to send up fresh growth, adds to the feeling that we are wandering through a living labyrinth."[20] Other fantasy artists second his thinking. In his *Fantasy Art Workshop*, John Howe emphasizes that rock forms the backbone of most post-Tolkien fantasy landscape illustration, and that trees often succeed best when they are drawn as rocks covered with bark.[21] In a visceral, visual, linguistic way, Tolkien's books became the prisms through which bright young readers encounter landscape in fiction and through which subsequent authors realize the importance of landscape.[22]

Tolkien grasped the aerial view as crucial in the nascent airliner age.[23] Corrupt birds and other evil creatures spy on hobbits from above, and giant eagles sometimes carry a hobbit who gains new, if overwhelming, insight into landscape. Dragons perform the same service in Ursula K. Le Guin's 1968 *A Wizard of Earthsea*. Tolkien, Le Guin, and other first-rate fantasy authors typically address young readers (and older ones) who know almost nothing of human flight beyond airline travel. They know nothing of the individual aerial perspective, nothing of balloon travel, nothing of 1900-era pedal-driven dirigibles flying above high schools, nothing of the 1950s promise of teenagers aloft over neighborhoods. Often they have never made a continental-scale road trip, never been low on gas, lost, misdirected, hungry, broken down, detoured, or exhausted and searching for a motel. They know only airliners, in-flight movies, and blurred color far below.

And they know the organized confusion of airports, the security checks emphasizing potential danger and disaster. For many young people, airports are key nodes, almost the only nodes they know as travelers.

Nodes must concern any inquirer into essential landscape. The isolated inn supplanted the isolated monastery, which for a thousand years put up travelers for the night, sheltering the poorest for free. But it is difficult to trace the development of what the British term a **public house**, a **pub**, from a simple tavern selling mead or wine (ale came late to the British Isles), a house with a room fitted with a plank across two kegs, the **bar**, and marked as a place retailing alcohol only by a branch fixed above the door, to an inn, a place offering rooms to sleep in rather than space on the tavern floor. Nor is it easy to distinguish the role of taverns and inns in the making of hamlets, villages, and towns, either in the mindset of inhabitants or in the view of travelers, suspicious and otherwise.

A **village** typically boasted a church building and churchyard, however small, and a **town** usually had a church and a regular if intermittent market typically licensed by authority, often authority above the lord of the nearest manor.[24] Villages and towns housed specialized craftsmen, above all blacksmiths who reshod the horses of locals and travelers alike. **Hamlet** is a troublesome term: educated people think instantly of Shakespeare's Danish prince. But it derives from the same roots as **home** and even boasts a diminutive, **hamel**. Misunderstood, awkward to define, and not often used by city people unless pejoratively or dismissively, its root is Old French, **hamelette**, and it arrived in the Norman Conquest, applying to tiny clusters of houses whose inhabitants worshipped in a church a long walk away. "Village" arrived in the same Norman ships: rooted in the Latin **villa**, designating a country house with adjacent peasant housing, it soon meant in law French something smaller than a town. The word forever wars with the French **ville** (designating a town or city) and **villain**, another Norman term denoting a rural, rustic, rude, low-born man of base character likely to prove criminal. After about 1815 **villain** was translated as **serf** (from the Old French **serf** rooted in the Latin **servus**, meaning **slave**), a word that scarcely existed in England before or after the Conquest.[25] But **villain** did, perhaps because the conquerors equated what they saw as the boorishness of English countrymen with a propensity for disobedience beginning with a base, dogged determination to keep speaking the English they used before 1066. "Villages" connoted places reached by bye-ways, places of narrow mindset. Crudeness suffuses usage. In urban slang, "village" conjures up the specter of idiots born of incest. Villages are close-minded, close, closed.

A town opens itself to strangers. Port towns might be more open, at least along the wharves, but any town acknowledges the importance of travelers and welcomes them. Hamlets and villages suspect strangers and often fear them. The difference originates in trade. Regular markets, seasonal or monthly, eventually weekly, require the mixing of locals—farmers especially, but also weavers and other craftsmen—and itinerant merchants. The marketplace itself, often an open area at the center of town intermittently filled with booths and stalls and unhitched wagons surrounded by permanent shops, demands also an effective order, the **peace of the market** typically symbolized by a large cross or other indication of order. Breach of the peace evoked stiff punishment, and preventing disorder preoccupied the local nobility, especially the lord of the manor in which the town existed and to whom it paid rent, the aldermen or other governors of the municipality, and the permanent or temporary law officers working the crowd.

Not surprisingly, towns walled for military purposes maintained walls and gatemen long after the prospect of civil war and foreign invasion ended. Guarded gateways enabled the sealing of the town after dark (including sealing in any would-be criminals) and controlling access from outside at any time. Criminals might enter masquerading as honest yeomen or travelers, but they risked being imprisoned by town walls and gates once they committed their crimes: robbing anyone meant the likelihood of the victim shouting for help, raising the **hue and cry** that follows the yelling of "Stop, thief!" and producing the immediate citizen pursuit, apprehension, and discipline peace officers worked hard to control (and sometimes stop).

At the same time, a village or town provided a church building, what the Romanian philosopher Mircea Eliade calls in his *The Sacred and the Profane* a **hierophany**, an intersection of the mundane world and heaven, something the prehistoric painters of caves knew.[26] The building and its yard existed in two realms and in divine service the realms fused, time and understanding shifting: the ecclesiastical year overlay the civil calendar just as divine timeliness on Sundays supplanted ordinary hours. But Christianity overlay the Old Religion like a veneer, and wise bishops and rectors struggled gently with that intersection, aware that what the Church called superstition pulsed strongly in everyday life. Every facet of the landscape existed in multiple planes. In churches priests baptized children with holy water, but on weekdays farmers baptized newborn calves with a handful of river water, mumbling age-old words they hoped guaranteed health. Before the Reformation, religion built monasteries and convents along with churches and chapels and cathedrals (many often oriented toward the sunrise): travelers erected crosses at places where they survived catastrophe, and markets proceeded peacefully under crosses symbolizing peace. Afterward Protestantism destroyed most monasteries and convents and altered church architecture; state-ordered national churches, especially the Church of England and its authorized version of the Bible in English and its *Book of Common Prayer*, structured national language, including landscape terminology.[27] It is easy to misjudge the importance of religion in shaping landscape, easy, for example, to misjudge the importance of pilgrimage in sending travelers onto roads and highways, appallingly easy to misjudge the role of the Church of England in shaping the English and American common law.[28] It is easy to misunderstand or deliberately devalue the everyday meaning of a village parish served by its rector in strengthening hope in times of plague or famine, to miss the effectiveness of ecclesiastical charity and ecclesiastical intervention on behalf of the poor, to miss how so many ways led from farmhouses to church. It is easy to forget why the church bell rings loudly as a wedding concludes or tolls loudly at the close of a funeral. The Prince of the Powers of the Air fears such sound and shies away, giving the new couple and the departing soul a strong start. A church bell celebrating a marriage, tolling a death, or merely noting passing hours spreads its aerial protection and peace over a village or town and all the outlying farmland where people can hear it.[29] It is far too easy for many inquirers into landscape to see a church and fail to comprehend that from bell towers and belfries booms noise across space, sound that shapes any perception of local landscape, even if the sound sometimes tolls only the time, not the weddings and funerals which exist outside it.

Church buildings, churchyards, and graveyards connect the mundane world, the ordinary landscape, with the divine. All are sacred structure and space, of course, but all are somewhat like wharves, between two realms, nowadays pushing even atheists along linguistic and especially lexicographical paths. **Holy** designates something other than **sacred**. No one says "the sacred Bible" or "the holy graveyard." And even the most dedicated of New Age cognoscenti understand that the margins of religion, faerie, and magic may front on extraterrestrial contact, perhaps soon.

It is equally easy to misjudge the survival of the Old Religion, especially the survival furthered by the new, as in the way the Church of England sanctified rogation days, those so important in maintaining property boundaries, astute forestry and horticulture, and responsible farming. Consider bridges and rivers. Old wisdom forbids urinating into rivers: the flowing water sweeps away the soul. Crossing a bridge in cloudy weather still worries some people: losing one's shadow in a river (when a cloud crosses the sun) means losing one's soul. Infants must not be carried aboard ferries or across bridges until about three months old lest the riverine force steal their souls. Mange can be cured if one throws the scab into the current. Jenny Greenteeth (a truly wicked nymph) snatches toddlers as they near river edges. Sin confessed onto bread tossed into rivers disappears, at least for a while. Folklore, superstition, however educated people think of it, rewards the closest scrutiny but still proves hard to study in English: the great studies of such topics across western Europe, the British Isles, and Iceland remain in languages other than English. Disciplined inquiry unnerves.

Before Christianity, bridge builders sacrificed humans at the edge of rivers, sometimes burying the bodies under the first piers: the custom lingered into the eighteenth century, felons being hanged at construction sites rather than in public squares. The first mortar of the Empire State Building was mixed with the blood of a rooster sacrificed especially for the purpose.

Folktale and now fantasy, science fiction, and postapocalyptic fiction emphasize the lost way, the broken road, the path which misleads in deep forest, the old road leading to ruins and worse, the demise of Bree and other towns, the collapse of cities, the grass (and worse) growing in streets. In the age of GPS and cell phones, getting lost still worries. It worries especially city dwellers who live in well-marked places well lit after nightfall, who dislike fog, who worry when color betrays. It raises awkward issues best studied after dark or in great snowstorms when cell phones fail. It makes reading Rolt's memory of safe dark alleys thought-provoking, even hard. Automobile headlights make driving into the deep dark easy, but on cloudy, moonless nights when everywhere shows only as dark, the old dark of old ways, the contemporary motorist often hunches down behind the glowing instruments and stares ahead with caution.

What then is wilderness on the dark road, the broken road headlights reveal as potholes, cracked asphalt, a rusted yellow diamond sign shot full of holes, trees blowing in the wind, leaves scattering across the way, sleet turning to freezing rain, maybe snow, cell phone reception patchy then gone? Is all that wilderness? No, not at all. With a good map beside one, the four-wheel-drive buttons glowing on the dashboard, the second gas tank filled, the emergency food and water and sleeping bag stowed away behind, a thermos of black coffee, the modern motorist pushes on. Dark and wind and rain and a broken road and a hitchhiker standing miles from buildings are not wilderness. Almost certainly not. Probably not.

Wilderness? What is wilderness now?

Well, **waal**, as the old New England Yankees say, stretching the word into a long, modulated groanlike tone, wilderness is something else.

Wilderness is the alternator light coming on.

Given a charged battery and radio and dashboard lights switched off, a contemporary automobile has about thirty minutes of operation left unless the driver switches off headlights and taillights too. In the words of one Harvard alumna, driving back roads across far upstate New York, in deep darkness, high wind, and rain at about 2:30 in the morning, blown-down branches littering a broken pavement, the alternator light suddenly blinking on indicates wilderness arrived, the lesson of a long-before lecture suddenly realized, made real, an automobile electrical system dying on a stretch of road in which her cell phone has no service, then the pretty car rolling to a stop.

And then a moment of memory, a lecture comment recalled. The driver-door storage pocket stuffed with snacks and gloves and tissue originated as something else. Before 1920 it originated as holster, the secure nesting place of a pistol. Wilderness can accomplish many things, even a momentary, fierce reevaluation of gun control thinking, a momentary reevaluation preceding a sudden, even more fierce desire to have a handgun snug in the hand.

Wilderness can be anywhere. It is everywhere, if usually latent or invisible. Especially on the road. The brightly lit inn, its roaring fire, the scent of hot food, the promise of a clean bed, all swirl beneath contemporary understanding of the cloverleaf motel, the lights of a village far ahead. But let the car break down, let the cell phone battery then die, and the night and storm and all the old things gather.

They gather fastest when one stands alone, wonders whether to leave the broken car and walk the broken road, or to sit and grow cold and await whatever traveler comes along—or whoever comes out of the dark woods beside the road.

Wilderness flows toward roads. Wilderness flows along roads. And a bit of preventive landscape analysis, especially as one walks or drives, sometimes proves useful when wilderness stalks. Even in cities, when great towers burn and fall, knowing how and where to move on foot, without electronic devices, proves useful. Thinking about walking home, walking across the Interstate Highway bridge, walking back streets toward lights and order, all such may prove useful one day.

Sometimes the bridge is out. Sometimes the motel is dark, the gas station closed for the night. Sometimes the village is abandoned. Sometimes an old, rusty pickup truck blocks the narrow, broken way.

The newly plowed field abuts the brushy fence line as most landscape abuts the ocean and the sandy beach: the sea seems always ready to move inland and the weeds and other wild plants seem always poised to bewilder the field.

8 FIELD

An ancient noun connoting human effort, **field** functions today in two ways, designating a constructed open area and a sort of theater of operations, **theater** designating not a playhouse but what military officers mean, an area of warfare. "An open space of land" according to Skeat's *Etymological Dictionary*, **field** comes from the Old English, Old Frisian, and Old Scandinavian **feld** and the somewhat later Dutch **veld**. In one way, its roots reach deeply into Old Germanic, to **felþuz**, as **feld** is somehow related to the Old English **folde**, naming land or earth. All the direct roots lie in what is now western Germany, reaching west (as in the Middle Dutch **velt** and later Dutch **veld**) and also north into modern Danish **felt** and Swedish **fält**. Far deeper is a Sanskrit root, **pṛthivī**, meaning earth, still evident in the Finnish **pelto** and the Russian **pole**. The Sanskrit root proved less resilient (or less evident) in the low-lying region of the Oder, Elbe, and Rhine.

One early meaning, open land as opposed to woodland, had become obsolescent toward the end of the sixteenth century and poetic by the end of the seventeenth, and another, connoting rural areas, had become poetic only when Shakespeare used it in *A Midsummer Night's Dream*: "in the town and the field you doe me much mischief."[1] A related meaning endures in fox hunting: **field** designates the area of the hunt and survives in the phrase **field sports**, which itself denotes outdoor games other than ones played in parks (baseball) or stadia (football and soccer). Another strong meaning, mostly used by specialists, is found in **coal field**, **oil field**, and **gold field**, terms related to military ones.

Warfare usage of **field** proves old, in writing dating to 1300 and meaning essentially a battlefield, even in duels fought on **fields of honor**. An equally important variant meaning centers on the whole region of a military campaign. Armies **in the field** govern themselves according to intent and chance and misadventure, moving over terrain utterly unlike the enclosed parade grounds of castles, keeps, and modern military bases. At the close of the nineteenth century, when romantic reformers created modern football as the moral equivalent of warfare, baseball tended to be played in **ball fields**, which shaped the early usage of **football field**. Contemporary emphasis on **level playing fields** ignores the unevenness of baseball terrain (the pitcher's mound) and excises soccer and football from golf, which extolls hills, traps, and other hazards. Football and golf are not field sports, at least not any more.

The root meaning endures as the strongest: "field" designates a piece of ground plowed more or less regularly for a crop (as in **hayfield, cornfield**, and **wheatfield**), manured or otherwise fertilized, sometimes weeded and—typically after harvest—sometimes grazed. Traditionally and often still, farmers enclose fields with fences, walls, and hedges, chiefly to keep out livestock: enclosure forms a crucial part of the concept. A plowed field proves rich in old and modern terminology from **furrow** and **land** to **contoured terrace**, revealing itself to any thoughtful inquirer, but an enclosed field awakens picture-book memories of bountiful crops, amber fields of grain, plenty.

As early as 1340 "field" denoted too an area of operation or observation, often of active study, in ways perhaps derived from military practice. As Francis Bacon remarked in 1626 of the increase of virtue, "it is a large field and to be handled by itself," so **landscape studies** is a large field.[2] Most scholars perceive its size as mocking any prudent, sensible effort at handling landscape by itself, and thus suggest that it is the study of everything outdoors (except perhaps in mid ocean or near the poles) jumbled together, and even claim it as the visible part of their own defined, manageable fields of study. Few scholars devote themselves to it exclusively. Those who do must be forever explaining it, often in terms likely to find favor with the inquirer.

Children, spouses, police officers (often encountered, always suspicious, then invariably friendly and frequently useful, they being professional observers who notice landscape by the way), almost everyone else encountered in the field, fellow scholars asked for supportive material or potential avenues (or broken paths) of inquiry, and above all deans and university presidents suspect **landscape studies** as designating an excuse for a ramble, maybe a slow drive down dirt roads, a long, thoughtful lark usually away from townscape and cityscape, adventure definitely beyond classrooms, libraries, and cell phone range, invariably examining ordinary places otherwise taken for granted, a trumped-up reason for field trips to beaches. No matter how often informed in short and lengthy memos, deans and university presidents routinely ask what **landscape studies** "actually means."

It means looking at built form outdoors—typically away from compact areas in which natural topography, surface features (trees especially), and natural systems have been well-nigh erased (as in urban cores), made purely ornamental (as opposed to trees planted as windbreaks, for example), or buried (in gutters or huge culverts)—and thinking about its history, present condition, and possible futures.

University administrators properly suspect it. They question it according to known frameworks, especially geography. But landscape is not topography, and certainly not cartography. Landscape studies' mixture of visual observation and subsequent archival research only confuses deans and presidents so busy exercising power they lack time and opportunity for walks.

But "landscape" misleads them. Typically they know the word as an adjective in art history, one defining a sort of painting of subjects most educated people consider beautiful. Often they know it as an adjective designating a type of architecture producing outdoor places sometimes considered beautiful (if not always pleasant) by almost everyone, especially the taxpayers who today tend to pay for what

eighteenth- and nineteenth-century British noblemen understood as **landscape gardens** or **parks**. As a noun, the word
befuddles the casual.

It betrays scholars struggling to make sense of "landscape studies" only because nineteenth-century German
geographers altered the meaning of **landschaft** in the name
of nation-building politics.[3]

In modern but poor-quality English-German dictionaries, "landscape" translates as "landschaft." Tracing the ways
linguists and lexicographers have translated "landscape" into
French, Spanish, Dutch, and Danish, and from those languages into English and German (the last is crucial) and
others proves a worthy educational effort, if tedious to the
point of drudgery. Between the middle of the nineteenth
century and the present, "landschaft" subtly dominated the
larger European (and American) scholarly concept of landscape while scarcely impacting the understanding of farmers, mariners, engineers, artists, noblemen, hikers, and
others directly involved in the creation and use of landscape
itself.

Nineteenth-century German imperialism and cartographic enterprise skewed all academic meaning of "landscape" beyond departments of art history and landscape
architecture.[4] In what is now northwest Germany originated
a usage German geographers championed in the name of the
Kaiser unifying former principalities. German mapmakers,
at the time the dominant cartographers in Europe, Britain,
and North America, seconded the effort. Two wars, still of
scant interest to most intellectuals, even those interested in
the origins of two subsequent world wars, focused German

national interest on the duchies of Schleswig and Holstein. In the First Schleswig War (1848–1851), Denmark and the emerging German state sparred over the fate of two duchies controlled by Denmark, one with a majority of German-speaking residents. In 1864 began the second war for control of the two duchies: it lasted some nine months, and demonstrated not only the superiority of railroads in modern warfare but the expanding might of the German army. At its close, a large number of Danish-speaking people found themselves Germans. Language, perhaps more importantly spoken language, immediately vexed German imperial authorities and German intellectuals: the vexation lingers in dairy regions of the United Kingdom and the United States. Holstein cows carry in their breed name something of the Danish-German conflict and something of a deeper issue many Americans recognize when asked.

Holstein cows seem somehow Dutch. Jersey cattle mark a trace of Norman Archipelago agriculture in modern English and American usage, but Holsteins grazing in a pasture produce a nagging crypto-memory of something outside schoolroom lessons. Children's books portray almost all cows as Holsteins, black-and-white cows, placid, stolid. The breed traces its origins to about 100 BC, when people displaced from present-day Hesse moved west with black cattle, met Frisians keeping white cattle, and following incivilities, began developing a dairy-and-beef breed which prospered on grass. The breed (and its breeders) prospered mightily in part because of the peacefulness of Frisians, who paid tribute in cattle and hides to the Roman Empire and thereafter to any overlord ruling them. Placidity split Frisia early between the Netherlands to the south and the duchies to the north along with parts of Germany near the Ems, and divided Old Frisian eventually into West Frisian and East Frisian. West Frisian continuously influenced English, especially that spoken just across the North Sea, but East Frisian became more and more German (especially in pronunciation). After 1864 Germany found itself facing the Germanizing of Danes suddenly within its borders, along with justifying its grabbing of Schleswig and Holstein in the first place, as well as dealing with East Frisians paying scant attention to modern German. It acted precisely.

Immediately German geographers and cartographers reimagined and remapped the occupied territories. Since much of the world used maps produced in Germany (but published in many languages), imagination (or visualization) and mapping proved global.[5] Essentially, German atlases became para-maps, the arbiter of disputes, the ultimate cartographic authority.[6]

Maps themselves evoke another meaning of "field," a surface on which something is portrayed. Coats of arms have fields on which colleges of heraldry inscribe charges, heraldry thus fusing one meaning of **field** with one of **shield**. Only lately have cartographers examined maps as fields of concepts and of power, and their links to other too easily accepted sources of cultural authority.[7]

German cartographers drew strength from related comprehensive reference sources. Hanns Bächtold-Stäubli's ten-volume *Handwörterbuch des deutschen Aberglaubens* (1927–1942) remains the premiere authority on European and British folk belief, including the incalculably rich

folklore of landscape and building.[8] It has never been translated into English. Maps, atlases, and allied reference works
reshaped perception of the new German nation and of pastures filled with cows renamed Frisians. American farm
books continue the effort, albeit visually.

A fragment of occupation and culture-changing effort
strengthened one denotation of "landschaft" by emphasizing
a traditional meaning of "land" as a small unit of government and "landschaft" as the national-administration overview of the unit through both its political identity and its
surface appearance.[9] It is almost impossible to translate the
fabricated German connotation into English, but in 1939
Richard Hartshorne tried, deciding finally that geographers
in the United States and throughout the British Empire
might think of the term as roughly synonymous with
region.[10] His book *The Nature of Geography: A Critical
Survey of Current Thought in the Light of the Past* emphasizes
that most Germans use "landschaft" as most English speakers use "landscape," somewhat vaguely, chiefly as designating the natural surface of the earth in a beautiful view
and—most of the time—built objects "imposed" on the
natural surface and, too, an image of wilderness or shaped
land, sort of wild scenery captured. But Hartshorne emphasizes too that for about a hundred years German geographers
had used it also distinctly, as meaning everything in a land
accessible to the senses. Hartshorne understood, almost viscerally, the gathering power of the German geographers,
who step by step focused on movable objects temporarily in
a place (ships in harbors, trains crossing fields, pedestrians
on roads) and on the immense power of sensory generators.

He noted pointedly that German geographers had begun defining the language heard in a place as one marker of landscape identity. By the late 1930s most thoughtful people knew the crises imminent in places like Alsace-Lorraine and how **lebensraum** (living space) figured in Nazi thinking about German speakers in Czechoslovakia, Ukraine, and elsewhere.[11] Hartshorne wanted English-speaking geographers to claim "landscape" for their own discipline, to define it more or less as did the German geographers, to present their thinking at international congresses, and in time to shape the ways educated people used the word. While especially irritated by American geographers using the term loosely, he considered that a new term might better suit all geographers. It must embrace "surface" (what German geographers called the **bild** of the land, a tricky concept involving both form and picture) and emphasize "a certain distinct and real aspect of an area," its "features." What he meant by **area** remains vague, and his vagueness only strengthened the hand of German geographers. Nonetheless, Hartshorne wanted a new term, and he liked "region."[12]

English lexicographers knew the deep past mined by German geographers after the middle of the nineteenth century. As early as 1516 **landgrave** appears in English denoting in Germany a count having jurisdiction over a territory split into several smaller sections each overseen by an inferior count. In the middle 1550s Englishmen wrote easily about **margraves** too, German military governors of border places, and knew of them in the Low Countries as well: "All such Rulers of townes or countries as are nere the sea, are called Mergraue, as at this day in Andwarpe," wrote Richard

Grafton in his 1568 *Chronicle at Large and Meere History of the Affayres of Englande.*[13] But while petty margraves ruled coastal spots and often ruled over emergency dike repairs with iron hands, English travelers and writers knew them as distinctly foreign, unlike the **graves** of Yorkshire and Lincolnshire, minor administrators elected by yeomen. In the east of England "grave" might be rooted in Old Norse (lexicographers really do not know), but it was obsolescent by about 1610: it never meant what **graf** came to mean in Germany, a count. In northwest Germany, in North Friesland, called **East Friesland** by the German authorities and cartographers, and in the conquered duchies especially, **deichgrafen**, minor noblemen exercising extraordinary powers in times of great storms, ruled the dikes that kept out the sea. The power of deichgrafen derived not only from the Kaiser and Prussian understanding of centralized authority, but from the absolute necessity of having someone in charge when dikes threatened to fail. New political order in East Friesland and the duchies rose above the need for power to confront the power of the sea in storm.

Englishmen rejected the entire formula of landgrafen ruling landschaften: the English local squire might be noble in dusty ways, but he was not lord of all he surveyed. In 1939, when Hartshorne wrote, "graf" had become a household word throughout the British Empire and the United States, across which flew the immense zeppelin named for the aircraft inventor Graf von Zeppelin. By then the duchies had had military governors and forced language alteration for some eighty years, and by then most thoughtful Britons and Americans knew the darkness ahead.[14]

World War II ended Hartshorne's effort to put geographers in charge of defining and practicing landscape studies.[15] Since 1945, geographers have made only a few efforts to claim the word "landscape" as theirs. It is a slippery word, a shape-shifter, and the few scholars serving it value its ability to mean exactly what will placate university administrators at any given moment.

World War I reinforced the casual, hands-in-the-pockets Victorian and Edwardian way of inquiring into landscape. In the years following the armistice, thousands of veterans walked off their stress, often accompanied by girlfriends and wives, using the British footpath system to enjoy the outdoors—and to wonder at what they found. Haphazard and happily, they and many others gentled onward a scarcely defined mode of inquiry.

More than ten years before Hartshorne tried to codify words and academic disciplines, Donald Maxwell set out on casual walks exploring the coast of Kent, sketchbook and compass shoved in one pocket, binoculars in another, always hoping to find a pub around lunchtime. His jewel-like *A Detective in Kent: Landscape Clues to the Discovery of Lost Seas* is one landmark in the misty field of landscape studies. Maxwell understood careful scrutiny of landscape as a sort of police work and individual landscape constituents—especially ones seemingly unimportant—as clues useful in figuring out the past. "Observation and accumulation of clues in a landscape are of immense value, but the deductions made from them must be tested and cross-examined by reference to other light—history, etymology, architecture, agriculture, or knowledge of local conditions," he notes in the preface, before insisting that on-the-ground looking around might contradict scholarly assertion. Chapters later, after summarizing the scholarly dispute about the first cultivation of Romney Marsh, he asks a question central to his book and answers it in terms of police work: "Now what are we detectives to do, when great authorities disagree? There is only one sound action, examine the evidence again and if we can find a clue as to who built the Rhee Wall, look for an adequate motive to explain such a work." In light of what he knew firsthand of inshore small-boat sailing and of archaeological work done at the site of Roman-built harbors, he decided that Roman military engineers had sited part of the existing wall but that most of it had been built long after. Before the diking and partial draining of the great marshes, galleys making land would have encountered a dangerous point of land where the wall might have originated. Maxwell imagines a Roman chart like a modern Admiralty one, marking the banks, **ripae**, and wonders if "it is significant that this western edge of the shingle marsh of Lydd is to this day named West Rype."[16] His entire book, illustrated with sketches and maps (the latter depicting what might have been), emphasizes educated, firsthand, sustained observation and ruminations about place names and local vocabulary.

Like J. R. R. Tolkien and other walkers of the postwar era, Maxwell reveled in etymology, especially that charging the work of the English Place-Name Society. In searching for the disappeared two mouths of the River Rother, one of which extended from Appledore to Hythe, he applied what he knew of estuarine silt movement and embanking to place names. "We must not miss the obvious, so we will notice in passing on that 'y' or 'ey' means island and that hithe is a wharf or landing-stage for ships," he explains of what he sketched. "Oxney is now six miles from the sea at its nearest point and West Hythe is now a mile and half from salt water," and Oxney is higher than the made land surrounding it. The movement of silt, mostly clay, might have formed a marshy island at the estuary mouth: any small-boat sailor might figure that out, especially after running aground. "The ancient British word for a marsh is 'ruimne' (possibly pronounced room). With 'y' or 'ey' tacked on for island we at last get 'ruimney' and Romney, the marsh island." In careful footnotes acknowledging other explanations for the name of the marsh, Maxwell makes clear that however strong they might be etymologically or in connection with period documents, they fail to fit the landscape precisely.[17] Moreover, etymologists appear united in a conviction that the root of **rhee**—**rhe** or **rhin**—means rapid or swift, suggesting something that runs, almost certainly an estuary current, and that the first part of the Rhee Wall existed in Roman times, before the diking and draining—what Maxwell calls the **inning**—of the low-lying coastal land. Deep in the reclaimed marshes he finds farm workers who know the names of places not on government maps, and whose pronunciation is local.

"The old people of the marsh still call Dymchurch Dime-church with a long 'I,'" Maxwell notes of distances along the dike, and muses that "the Norman-French dime is a tenth and is used to-day in France for tithe," which fact may give light. Other facts give light in the sun-washed marsh, even when rain charges in. Here and there a gable recalls the settlement of mid-sixteenth-century Protestant Dutch refugees expert in weaving and equally expert in making land, what Maxwell calls **polder** before explaining the making. His book moves along like a contemporary police-procedural mystery novel, tracing his irregular path, false starts, circular hikes, quests for information in archives and libraries, "dead reckoning of landscape observation," and his teasing the spatial history of a place out of details and seeming unimportant landscape features: "A more impressive little bit of landscape I do not think you could find, if you can see it, not as a marsh and a few ditches, but as an old sea-coast." All it takes, he demonstrates, is a thoughtful walk and bit of luck. "The slanting light of the morning casting the shadows of small willows across this little cutting made it seem more than ever likely to have been a place of ships," he says of finding "a green ghost of other days," a tiny dock built for Roman galleys moving up the lost Wantsum River, ready to discharge cargo at the fringe of the empire.[18]

A Detective in Kent subverts the deepening specialization of early twentieth-century academic research. "What we want therefore for the equipment of the landscape detective is not so much highly specialized knowledge of one subject as an intelligent correlation of slight knowledge of many subjects," Maxwell argues at the start of his first investigation. But to him knowledge is more outlook than range of facts. "An ideal landscape detective would be a superman who knows something of the outlook of a philologist, historian, sailor, engineer, architect, military strategist, student of comparative religion, geologist, and arborist," he opines.

"He must also possess a savour of humour, common sense, observation, and a knowledge of human nature." In 1929 Maxwell identified the equipment, outlook, and straightforward commonsensical approach that enlivened the work of subsequent inquirers.[19]

In the same years, Vaughn Cornish explained both the ground rules of British scenery aesthetics and the best ways of photographing the British landscape. His 1932 *The Scenery of England: A Study of Harmonious Grouping in Town and Country* predates his *Scenery and the Sense of Sight* by only three years. His books define why so many Britons so valued certain components of larger landscapes and why so many tourists, especially Americans, arrive to enjoy, paint, and photograph them. In 1939 appeared Julian Tennyson's *Suffolk Scene: A Book of Description and Adventure* detailing why Constable painted in certain spots that still satisfied and delighted Englishmen.[20] The books—and the thinking underlying them—became important in World War II, for they helped explain why Britons fought. As Cornish gently implied in his 1943 *The Beauties of Scenery: A Geographical Survey*, the larger British landscape symbolized core components of British freedom. In this period the countryside preservation movement and the footpath preservation movement evolved into important political forces, ones which shape Prince Charles's 2010 *Harmony: A New Way of Looking at Our World*. Pedestrian scale, open views over agricultural land, water (salt or fresh) more or less everywhere: all components of traditional British scenery aesthetics, Charles uses them in his argument against much modern building, understanding them as tested elements in sustainable,

earth-friendly, futurist design. His book irritates many
architects and urban designers, as he knew it would, but
entrances many deep-pocketed real estate developers cogni-
zant of ideas already manifest in yoga practice and other
twenty-first-century culture.

Military aerial photography shaped landscape studies in
the 1930s too. Images made above Britain for reconnaissance
training purposes revealed palimpsests atop palimpsests.
While not visible at ground level, the overlay proved real
enough. Archaeologists began preliminary exploration and
made discovery after discovery. Just after the war, however,
on-the-ground military experience shaped the work of a
handful of scholars changed by battlefield discovery and by
aerial imagery. Knowing or suspecting what might be over the
next hill, especially if intelligence services or captured enemy
maps suggested nothing important, often meant life, death, or
disaster. In subsequent peacetime, military experience ener-
gized the work of a handful of academics young enough to
appreciate the disturbing vision of aerial photography.

In Britain W. G. Hoskins (1908–1992) and Maurice
Beresford (1920–2005) demonstrated the worth of landscape
study to both fellow scholars and the educated general public.
Each published widely. Beresford's 1951 *Lost Villages of
Yorkshire* emphasized what complexity lay forgotten under
farm fields: it opened on a range of books including his 1990
Wharram Percy: Deserted Medieval Village. Hoskins worked
at a larger scale. His 1955 *The Making of the English Landscape* made clear a similar complexity nationwide, something
he in time introduced in a series of BBC Television shows
and in subsequent books, especially *Old Devon* in 1966.[21]

Together they made discoveries which won the respect of scholars in many fields, and together they emphasized the need of good shoes and sandwiches. In his 2001 *Landscape Detective: Discovering a Countryside*, Richard Muir emphasizes the enduring triumph of their approach in Britain.

In the United States, John Brinckerhoff Jackson, in wartime a colonel in army intelligence who worked behind enemy lines, returned home to New Mexico, ranched, and founded *Landscape*, a scholarly magazine at first focused on the American Southwest and northern Mexico. His *American Space: The Centennial Years, 1865–1876* in 1972 confirmed what risk-taking deans at Harvard University and the University of California at Berkeley hoped: looking carefully at landscape over time often raises issues most scholars miss. In subsequent books he angled the field toward what he called "vernacular" landscape, the one made and used by most people most of the time, not the great buildings and gardens beloved of historians of architecture and landscape architecture. Jackson walked a lot but often traveled on a motorcycle, explaining that the American landscape, more vast than British and European ones, demanded a vehicle somewhat like a horse.[22]

While few scholars occupy chairs in the history of landscape—despite receiving pleasant postcards from afar, deans remain suspicious of a generalist field involving long field trips—many scholars brush against the discipline. Art historians sometimes delve into the landscape before scanning easels, as do Kenneth Clark in *Landscape into Art* (1949), Wolfgang Stechow in *Dutch Landscape Painting of the Seventeenth Century* (1980), Louis Hawes in *Presences of Nature:*

British Landscape 1780–1830 (1982), Christopher Brown in *Dutch Landscape: The Early Years, Haarlem and Amsterdam, 1590–1650* (1986); and Susan McGowan and Amelia F. Miller in *Family and Landscape: Deerfield Homelots from 1671* (1996). Other scholars examine the theoretical and literary nature of landscape concepts: Chris Fitter's *Poetry, Space, Landscape: Toward a New Theory* (1995) and Melanie L. Simo's *Literature of Place: Dwelling on the Land before Earth Day 1970* (2005) offer a splendid introduction. In *Landscape, Literature, and English Religious Culture, 1660–1800: Samuel Johnson and the Languages of Natural Description* (2004), Robert J. Mayhew emphasizes the enduring, powerful impact of religion on landscape perception. Yi-Fu Tuan works differently: in *Topophilia: A Study of Environmental Perception, Attitudes, and Values* (1974), *Landscapes of Fear* (1979), and other books, he analyzes ways people envision and evaluate landscape. William Cronon's *Changes in the Land: Indians, Colonists, and the Ecology of New England* (1983) exemplifies an approach shaped by ecology, and four books reveal the power of authority in the making of landscape: David Blackbourn's 2006 *The Conquest of Nature: Water, Landscape, and the Making of Modern Germany*, Joanna Guldi's 2012 *Roads to Power: Britain Invents the Infrastructure State*, Christopher L. Pastore's 2014 *Between Land and Sea: The Atlantic Coast and the Transformation of New England*, and Anthony Acciavatti's 2015 *Ganges Water Machine: Designing New India's Ancient River*. But in the end the field is peopled by few scholars devoted to it, and those who are like to keep it small, alert, active, nimble, and beyond the purview of academic authority.

Fields and disciplines have cliques and disputes, chair-
men, reports, and theories, and often clash with other fields
and disciplines. Landscape studies, perhaps because its few
scholars do their own fieldwork, somehow avoids the
bureaucratic impedimenta sedentary scholars and hangers-
on love. Unorganized, unafraid of mishap and getting lost,
often appearing ignorant especially in front of locals, the few
do what anyone can do—move along slowly, look, listen,
think, and try to learn later about what turned up.

Anyone can do it. With some determined effort.

It is situated in grass land over two miles from the sea. It stands on the spot of our first imaginary island *and the name of the farm is Belle Isle.*

In *A Detective in Kent* (1929), Donald Maxwell urged readers to wander outdoors alertly, to notice details, to never forget the depths of meanings implicit in old place names and other terms, and to find good lunches. Author's collection.

9 AWAY

Landscape connotes now some mix of the wild, the agricultural, and the structured (if structured means fitted with buildings), with the wild always pushing and shoving and changing. In the minds of many Americans, "landscape" designates something away from predominantly shaped built form (the latter being the space and structure ornamented with trees and plants in planters, sometimes impervious to rain, usually and continuously controlled—and heated, cooled, and illuminated by mechanism). It means something other than **townscape** and especially **cityscape**.

"It has been observed many times that the notion of landscape is an urban construct and that those who live outside city walls do not differentiate between an all-encompassing nature and a backdrop for human action," asserts Alberto Manguel in his *City of Words*.[1] For Manguel, who lives in a sixteenth-century house (graced with 30,000 books) in rural France, landscape itself shapes cultural—and especially literary—inquiry, even repeated rereading of

Kenneth Grahame's *The Wind in the Willows*. Landscape matters to Manguel. Where he lives, few signs address strangers, or anyone else. Where he lives is not city, not cityscape, not much signed or marked or mapped. To many intellectuals, perhaps to most city people, he is outside city walls indeed. But he is not uncomfortable, even after dark. His locale, his landscape, is pleasant to visit, somehow energizing and calming. Where he lives might as well be Maine. "Vacationland," read the license plates of the northeasternmost American state. Out there. Away. Away from something rarely defined. But away. Relaxing. Restorative. By the sea.

Among the many draws of the seacoast, especially the low-lying seacoast of broad, sandy beaches, surely the calming power of the strand proves important. At the beach people relax, unbend, open themselves to elemental forces. Anne Morrow Lindbergh gets close to it all in her *Gift from the Sea*, but too few men read her book. She writes of opening herself to the marge, taking it in, feminine terminology off-putting to men determined to penetrate mystery. On the beach the inquirer finds the essential landscape. The inquirer finds too guzzles and—given awareness and effort—perhaps the word **guzzle** itself.

But the typical inquirer finds few signs. Cities are almost entirely signs. It is impossible for a literate urban walker to read aloud all the signs encountered on a casual walk. In a way Manguel almost certainly does not intend, cities *are* words, and mostly advertisements. To survive in cities, the typical person learns to ignore almost all signage as he or she ignores almost all ambient noise and conversation. The educated person learns to ignore a great deal more.[2]

On the beach words matter a bit differently, perhaps especially to the bikinied or the otherwise nearly nude, walking and relaxing and noticing, electronic devices and other distractions left behind. Signs are few. Seaward are none, parallel to the surf are none, and only (sometimes) inland, beyond the landward edge of the sand, do signs trap the eye. Walking the beach without cell phone (and certainly without an old unabridged dictionary and this little book) gentles the inquirer into examining the edge of the land and the edges of landscape and landscape nomenclature.

In 1920 *Landscape Architecture* published a fragment of book manuscript the great landscape architect Frederick Law Olmsted (1822–1903) never completed. Near the end of his life, the designer of Central Park in New York, and of so many other spaces almost everyone considers enduring, evolving examples of design genius, began to write about considering landscape. "The Disuse of Older Landscape Words and Terms" introduces what he explored as he rode horseback across the American South just before the Civil War. Words matter. The fragment lists **strath**, **holme**, **dell**, **hithe**, **rand**, **knapp**, **floss**, **comb**, **brant**, **linn**, and others, among them **messuage**, **garth**, and **cottage**. Olmsted noted that westward-moving pioneers "have taken up words from the older Spanish and French pioneers." And he argued incisively that knowing the richness of such words should matter in the coming twentieth century, when "cottage" had come to denote a grandiose beach house.[3] One of the most visual and spatially competent designers of any age, he cherished words as much as anything he saw, envisioned, and built.

In his 1806 *Compendious Dictionary of the English Language*, Noah Webster defines **swosh** as "a narrow or shallow channel" and notes brusquely, "Carolina." His *American Dictionary of the English Language*, the 1828 unabridged dictionary which established his reputation as the great champion of American English, omits **swosh** as a headword. Instead it defines **swash**. One meaning, "a blustering noise," it condemns as vulgar. Another it offers without etymology: "impulse of water flowing with violence. In the southern states of America, *swash* or *swosh* is a name given to a narrow sound or channel of water lying within a sand bank, or between that and the shore. Many such are found on the shores of the Carolinas." The *American Dictionary* omits **swish**. It omits **susurrus** too. Why the *Century Dictionary* planted mangroves in swashes no one knows. But on the edge of the land, back to what is most definitely neither land nor landscape, back to the sea, the inquirer confronts the essentials of landscape and moves inland. Hopefully gently, hopefully deliberately. Perhaps over a seawall. Perhaps into an old dictionary like Richardson's *New Dictionary of the English Language,* which defines "landscape" as **coast**. Perhaps into the bibliography following these last pages.

Just as the sea is always whispering (or crashing loudly, perhaps **swashing**), so the inquirer into essential landscape discovers that landscape whispers too, not always clearly, often in old or ancient or dialect words, sometimes in ones not in new dictionaries. Where people shaped or shape land adjacent to tide water provides some of the richest vocabulary, but in the end, or at the edge of the end, essential landscape and landscape terminology reveal a lone fact.

Landscape is fragile. And the climate changes now, as it did when Dunwich drowned. Anyone who notices understands what children on the beach learn as the tide reaches for sandcastles. Natural forces still rule, even over castles.

At the edges things clash and merge. One way of beginning a lifelong avocation is to look closely at the beach, then the alongshore landscape, to wonder at docks and yards and paths, to ask always the names of what comes to mind as one walks slightly inland, to look under bridges, to walk in the dark, to ask about color, to think always about what it means to fly as contemporary airline passengers fly, not as teenagers once flew, to find lunch and remember that the food came from a farm, usually a farm in fly-over land, and to think always of home and whatever home means. **Landscape** designates something so complex and rich and overwhelming it is best not to take one's inquiries too seriously. Inquiring into landscape is often an excuse for a walk, a rewarding walk.

This book is no field guide. Close it now, put it down, and go.

Ebbing tide accentuates the detail-choked messiness in the margin, the abandoned marine railway and ruined pilings, the wall at the upland edge of the marsh, the plank and path leading toward more permanent shaped form. JRS

NOTES

INTRODUCTION

1. West Frisian terms and etymologies are from Doornkaat Koolman, *Wörterbuch der ostfriesischen Sprache*. See especially the entry for "schâp," noting especially the variant pronunciation "schup." Dutch terms are defined according to the *Groot woordenboek der Nederlandse taal*. See also De Vries and De Tollenaere, *Etymologisch woordenboek*. Pronunciations and sometimes meanings may differ in North Frisian, something made more or less clear in all these works.

2. Except where otherwise noted, *Oxford English Dictionary* entries shape all definitions and etymologies of English words cited here. But see also Halliwell, *Dictionary of Archaic and Provincial Words*.

3. Jones, *Steady Trade*, 176.

4. As demonstrated by Wright, *Sources of London English*. For centuries after the Norman Conquest, terms used along estuaries and in other alongshore places, including those brought from across the North Sea, perplexed educated Englishmen, especially clerks writing in Latin.

5. Liszka and Walker, *The North Sea World in the Middle Ages* introduces the richness of cultural contact and linguistic transfer.

6. Thoen and Van Molle, *Rural History in the North Sea Area* makes clear the scale and complexity of medieval agricultural innovation and cross-sea transfer of expertise.

7. In the 1970s Ype Poortinga discovered not only a wealth of folk tales among elderly West Frisians living in old-age homes but a wealth of words unknown to white-collar people who had never heard of the folktales that Steven de Bruin collected in the 1930s or those the aged women remembered forty years later. See, for example, Poortinga's *It fleanend skip* and *De ring fan it ljocht*. See also Mak, *Island in Time*, 224–240.

8. See, for example, Howell, *Lexicon Tetraglotton* (1660), under "bank" (which gives "shelf").

9. Milton, "Comus," in *Poetical Works*, 32.

10. Jones, *Working Thin Waters*, 61, deals with shelving land and shell tipping.

11. Jones, *Short Voyages*, 116–118, uses the term "shelf" explicitly in connection with the oyster fishery.

12. As Schäfer shows in *Early Modern English Lexicography*, the *OED* misses many terms (and incorrectly or incompletely defines others) due to its traditional reliance on literary texts, something Wright, *Sources of London English* corroborates: see esp. 2–5.

13. Rees, *Cyclopaedia* offers far more detailed articles on landscape and engineering matters (with sumptuous illustrations) than do contemporaneous editions of the *Britannica*, but it is not paginated.

14. Ibid., under "Canal."

15. Estimating surf height from seaward proves as hard today as ever; see United States Navy, *American Practical Navigator*, 662.

16. King, *Sea of Words*, 75.

17. On the pronunciation of "tackle" in American English, see especially *Webster's New International Dictionary*.

18. Waters, *The Rutters of the Sea*, ii–xiv, 1–56, and passim. See also Howse and Thrower, *Buccaneer's Atlas*, 8–36 and passim.

19. "Roader," a New England and Pacific Northwest term for a horse good for speed over roads, is sometimes pronounced "rudder." See *Dictionary of American Regional English* under "rudder."

20. On ripples in sand exposed at low tide, see Cornish, *Ocean Waves*.

21. The first is reproduced in Brown, *Dutch Landscape*, 148; the second in Wiemann et al., *Die Entdeckung der Landschaft*, 174.

22. In the Great Blizzard of 1978, the pattern of protection revealed itself on the coast of Scituate, Massachusetts; it did so again in the No Name storm of 1991. See Stilgoe, *Alongshore*, 45–71.

23. See "landschap" and "polder" in De Vries and De Tollenaere, *Nederlands etymologisch woordenboek*; De Vries and De Tollenaere, *Etymologisch woordenboek*; and *Groot woordenboek der Nederlandse taal*. See also Dugdale, *History of Imbanking and Drayning of Divers Fennes and Marshes* (1662).

1 MAKING

1. Eyges, *Practical Pilot*, 92–94. This is the only pilotage manual aimed at small-boat mariners eschewing electronic gadgetry.

2. Mellor, *Art of Pilotage*, 7–55, emphasizes the need for disciplined observation.

3. O'Brien, *Sea-Boats*, 168–171. O'Brien advises not attempting such landings; so does the Royal Navy: see Admiralty, *Manual* 1:218–219.

4. Barnes, *Dinghy Cruising*, 19.

5. Ibid.

6. Mulville, *Terschelling Sands*, 48, 51–52, 54–55.

7. Karlsson, *Mother Sea*, 246–247.

8. Returning to land gets short shrift in many how-to books about small-boat pilotage; see, for example, Dye, *Dinghy Cruising*, esp. 118–120, 165–166.

9. On Civil War balloons, see Wigglesworth Papers, MS N-114, June 17, 1862, Massachusetts Historical Society, Boston (the author of the document is unidentified).

10. On rural American ballooning, see Landrum, *Historical Sketches*, 32–41.

11. Quoted in Linn, *History of Centre and Clinton Counties*, 131–132.

12. Coombs, "Young Crusoes," 521.

13. Wise, "Experiments," 90.

14. Eddy, "Photographing from Kites," esp. 86–87.

15. De Beauffort and Dusariez, "Aerial Photographs" offers a glimpse of the hobby; Cottrell, *Kite Aerial Photography* explains modern practice.

16. See, for example, Duryea, "Universal Road."

17. On dirigibles in general, see Eckener, *Die Amerikafahrt des "Graf Zeppelin,"* and Role, *L'étrange histoire*. Women flew routinely in dirigibles from the beginning, but not in airplanes.

18. "Dragon-fly" offers a useful pictorial explication of the airplane as modernity.

19. Langewiesche, *I'll Take the High Road*, 101, 40, 18–19.

20. See, for example, Charles Lindbergh, *We*.

21. Lindbergh, *North*, 48–49, 240.

22. Markham, *West*, 34, 67–68.

23. Langewiesche, *I'll Take the High Road*, 18.

24. Lindbergh, "Airliner to Europe," 45. See also Morand, *Air indien*, on flying over South America circa 1930.

25. See, for example, Holme, "Influence."

26. Chiles, "Flying Cars," esp. 146.

27. Cuban, *How Teachers Taught*, 48.

28. Chamberlin, "Shall We Let Our Children Fly?," esp. 15–16. See also Brucker, "Airplane."

29. On tiny helicopters circa 1970, see Brown, "How You Can Own and Fly Your Own Whirlybird": in its back pages, *Popular Science* routinely ran small ads for such machines. They did fly and became the bane of rural women sunbathing nude, something that presages drone video-making.

30. For a 1940 example, see Berlin, "Robert Noyce," which describes an aircraft Noyce, aged twelve, built with his fourteen-year-old brother. The article includes a photograph.

31. I have tried photographing the landscape from a hang-glider and learned the results of distraction.

32. Morgan and Lester, *Graphic Graflex*, 341.

33. An especially penetrating analysis is Downes, *Sleeping Island*.

34. Tomeï, *De bovenkant van Nederland*, 9–10, 12–13.

35. Gamble, *Timewalkers*, ix, 236–237, 139–141, 15–16, x.

36. Dickson, *Dawn of Belief*, 14–15, 23–24.

37. Ibid., 118–119, 204–205, 120.

38. Fireworks here prove important; aerial fire catches the eye still: see Werrett, *Fireworks*.

39. Neev and Emery, *Destruction of Sodom*, 98–99, 127–131, 141. See also Grinsell, "Christianisation," and Simpson, "God's Visible Judgments."

40. Violet, *Solitary Journey*, 65–66.

41. Rolt, *Landscape with Machines*, in *Landscape Trilogy*, 31–32.

42. Ibid., 32.

43. Until World War II, the authors of children's books directed attention to such issues: see Petersham and Petersham, *Story Book of Trains*, and Lent, *Clear Track Ahead*.

44. Volcanoes emit light too, of course.

45. Oliver and Lancashire, *Blokes Up North*, 136.

46. Bachelard, *Psychoanalysis of Fire* is a superb introduction.

47. Mitchell, *Reveries of a Bachelor*, esp. 17–108.

48. Abbey, *Desert Solitaire*, 15, 143, 13–14.

49. Beacon Street in Boston, Massachusetts, takes its name from a hilltop fire lit to guide travelers moving on land.

50. Stilgoe, *Old Fields*, 157–164, 309–359.

51. Went, "Blue Hazes."

52. Minnaert, *Light and Color*, 259–261, 290.

53. Ibid., 360–362.

54. Brusatin, *History of Colors*. Goethe, *Italian Journey*, 73–74.

55. Hoffman, *Visual Intelligence*, 130, 134.

56. Hinchman, *Trail*, 24–25, 103.

57. Ibid., 122–125, 150, 15, 88–89, 92.

58. Stilgoe, *Outside Lies Magic*. See also Solnit, *A Field Guide to Getting Lost*.

59. Casson, *Priceless Art*, 35, 86–87, 160–161. See, for example, Milgram, "Experience of Living in Cities." Many police officers prize the observational skills their teachers ignored or deprecated.

60. Grose's 1785 *Classical Dictionary of the Vulgar Tongue* is also useful.

2 CONSTRUCTS

1. Clarke, *East Coast Passage*, 38.

2. Greenwood, *Once Aboard*, 39, 48, 42, 16. Many editors would not let pass his vulgarities, I suspect.

3. Clarke, *East Coast Passage*, 172, 195.

4. See, for example, Roupnel, *Histoire de la campagne française*.

5. Some scholars wish it were: see, for example, Muir, "Conceptualizing Landscape."

6. All devote space to disputes too often condensed in the *OED*, and all figure in this book: see, for example, Partridge, *Origins* under "beck" compared against Onions, *Oxford Dictionary of English Etymology*.

7. Ansted, *Dictionary of Sea Terms*, defines alongshore terms well; see also Waters, *Severn Tide*.

8. Thornton, *Scholar in His Study*, addresses such differences brilliantly; see esp. xi, 6, 15–18, and passim.

9. Butcher, *Lowestoft*, 12–13. In fairness to urban designers, scores are rare in American cities and towns.

10. See, for example, Boileau and Picquot, *New Dictionary*, under "landscape."

11. Olwig, "Recovering the Substantive Nature of Landscape" is a good introduction to recent thinking.

12. De Vries and de Tollenaere, *Nederlands etymologisch woordenboek*, under "landschap." See also their *Etymologisch woordenboek* under "landskep."

13. Willinsky, *Empire of Words*, esp. pp. 92–127, 195–198.

14. Manguel, *Library at Night*, explores the personal library as a sort of landscape.

15. Halliwell, *Rambles*, esp. 181–184: Halliwell was often off the road.

16. Halliwell, *Dictionary*, under "acker."

17. The twirling seems to have been something other than a bore: see Stilgoe, *Shallow-Water Dictionary*, 28–30.

18. Jones, *Jersey Norman French*, 7–12.

19. Lukis, *Outline*, 1–6; see also Jones, *Jersey Norman French*, 45–49. In 1960 Peter Kennedy recorded many archipelago terms: see his *La Collection Jersiaise*.

20. The Baltic island of Bornholm offers a comparative example: see Thygesen and Blecher, *Swedish Folktales*, esp. xiii–xxix.

21. Vocabulary from De Garis, *Dictionnaire* and Lukis, *Outline*.

22. In Hugo, *Toilers* [1888], 275, the line reads: "is a combination of what is called in France *épi*."

23. See Hugo, *Toilers* [1992], vi, xix–xxii, 349, 312, 439–440, 89–92. For an example of a nineteenth-century translation, see Hugo, *Toilers* [1888], which eliminates "La mer et le vent."

24. Lukis, *Outline*, 58.

25. Kaplan, *Coming*, 159–160.

26. Ibid., 160, 161–162. Conrad grew up speaking Polish; his superb English perhaps results from its being his beloved adopted language.

27. Nicholls, *Swahili Coast*, 9.

28. Freeman-Grenville, *East African Coast*, 27, 31.

29. Boyd-Bowman, *Léxico* proves magical to anyone traveling in Latin American back country: *From Latin to Romance* spices any travel in northwest France: "Regional Origins" pioneered much subsequent work by Latin American philologists, as my Latin American students attest. See also his "A Sample of Sixteenth-Century 'Caribbean' Spanish Phonology," in Milan, *1974 Colloquium*, 1–11.

30. In the quiet of the dusty gas station bay I listened carefully.

31. The folio maps in Kurath, *Linguistic Atlas* demonstrate variety still current in the region: the pronunciation of "boat" is especially revealing.

32. Burke, *Popular Culture* offers a lucid introduction to class distinction after about 1500.

33. Bellenden, *Livy's History*, 449; Crouch, *English Empire*, 4:70. Asking people from Jackson Hole about the name of their town is fun, especially aboard the Martha's Vineyard steamer (and the distinction between those who call the vessel the **steamer** and those who call it the **ferry** rewards close attention).

34. See, for example, Karlsson, *Pully-Haul*, 113: the translator leaves the word in Swedish.

35. Oliphant, *Death Served Up Cold*, 1–3.

36. Bartlett, *Dictionary*, 51.

37. De Vere, *Americanisms*, 89.

38. Clapin, *New Dictionary*, 86; see also her *Dictionnaire canadien-français* under "bois."

39. Cooper, *Bee-hunter*, 138. *Dictionary of American Regional English*, 475, suggests the term did not survive west of Indiana.

40. Sorden, *Lumberjack Lingo*, 87–88.

41. Irving, *Tour*, 135.

42. Clarke, *East Coast Passage*, 157.

43. See Manguel, *Library at Night*, 276–278, and Maillet, *Rabelais et les traditions populaires en Acadie.*

44. Landscape architect Matthew John Brown of Fogo Island, Newfoundland, introduced this word to me in December 2014.

45. Bradford, *Mediterranean*, 242–243.

46. For an introduction to Graves's poetry, see *Selected Poems*.

47. Roget, *Thesaurus*, sec. 350. See also Roget, *New Thesaurus*, sec. 350, which adds "tedge."

48. Hüllen, *English Dictionaries*, emphasizes traveler use of topical dictionaries.

49. Aitchison, *Words in the Mind*, esp. 12–13.

50. Ansted, *Dictionary of Sea Terms*, deals well with the two terms.

51. Spenser, *Faerie Queene*, I.i.13. See also Skeat, *Etymological Dictionary*, under "gate," and Shipley, *Dictionary*, under "runagate."

52. Stilgoe, *Old Fields*, esp. 221–250. See also Stilgoe, *Metropolitan Corridor*, 335–346.

53. On the contemporaneous background of their search, see Mowat, *West Viking*.

54. Whiteley, *Northern Seas*, 217–220.

55. In regions where industrialism has failed, this proves especially apt. Old men grieve for the abandoned factories in which they once worked, often seeing them as monuments to capitalist betrayal.

56. Brace, *Between Wind and Water*, 61–62.

57. Ibid., 62. On abandoned landscape and its meanings to locals and newcomers, see Stilgoe, *Old Fields*.

58. Cassidy et al., *Dictionary of American Regional English* cites it: few other dictionaries do.

59. Brace, *Between Wind and Water*, 69–72.

60. Béjoint, *Lexicography of English*, 129–162, is especially insightful on these volumes.

61. The volume changes bicycle dynamics, especially on broken pavement.

62. See, for example, Béjoint, *Lexicography of English*, 21, 83, 203.

63. On the general background in the United States, see Friend, *Development of American Lexicography*.

64. Richardson, *New Dictionary*, under "land" (1190).

3 ECHOES

1. An old but solid introduction to European voyages is Newton, *Great Age of Discovery*. See also Williams, *Great South Sea*.

2. Park, *Dictionary of Environment* under "land."

3. Smyth, *Sailor's Word-Book*, under "land" and "ledge."

4. Defoe, *Robinson Crusoe*, 1:47–50.

5. Hugo, *Toilers* [1992], 12, 236–237, 144, 216–217.

6. Stilgoe, *Lifeboat*, 23, 42–47, 63–64.

7. Listening to young children during art museum field trips proves instructive: often they remark on wind.

8. Wells, *War in the Air*, 194.

9. Shakespeare, *Winter's Tale*, IV.iv.

10. The statute is 36 Edward III (1362). Bothwell, *Age of Edward III*, makes clear the powerful heritage of Norman feudal thinking.

11. Musson, *Medieval Law* is a solid introduction to a rich, nuanced subject.

12. Coke, *First Part of the Institutes of the Laws of England* is most useful in terms of land and land tenure.

13. Black, *Law Dictionary*, 1064–1065, 1183, 132.

4 HOME

1. Shakespeare, *Henry the Sixth, Part 2*, IV.ii.

2. For the Charter of the Forest, see Rothwell, *English Historical Documents*, 3:337–340; see also Dietze, *Magna Carta*; Thomas, *Historical Essay*; and Howard, *Magna Carta*.

3. See for example, Plucknett, *Statutes*, and Turner, *Judges, Administrators, and the Common Law*.

4. Coke, Seymane 5 *Co. Rep.* 91 (1604): see Coke, *The First Part*.

5. Poets and others often get legal sources and words wrong: see Rigby, *Chaucer in Context*, esp. 90–99.

6. Blackstone, *Commentaries*, vol. 4, ch. 16.

7. On bows and other householder arms, see Powicke, *Military Obligation*.

8. *Statutes of the Realm*, 4:804–805.

9. Shipley, *Dictionary*, under "husk."

10. Jones, *Howard Mumford Jones*, 279.

11. For an introduction, see Wood, *Hearth*.

12. Blackstone, *Commentaries*, vol. 4, ch. 16.

5 STEAD

1. Jackson, "Ghosts at the Door," in Zube and Zube, *Changing Rural Landscapes*, 41, 43.

2. Andrew, *Noble Lyfe and Natures of Bestes*, n.p.

3. Jackson, "Ghosts at the Door," 43–44.

4. This was the day King Philip IV of France arrested the Knights Templar and disbanded the order: its stark horror endured as a symbol of precipitous bad fortune.

5. Boissonnade, *Life and Work*, 284–285.

6. Zinsser, *Rats*, 88–90. See also Abel, *Die Wüstungen*, esp. pp. 12–59.

7. Sticker, *Abhandlungen aus der Seuchengeschichte* remains a detailed study. See also Laslett, *World We Have Lost*, 123–129.

8. For a general introduction to the context of the word, see Häberle, *Wüstungen*.

9. Grimm and Grimm, *Annotated* is the best translation.

10. Roux, *Territoire* is a useful introduction. See also Beresford, *Lost Villages*.

11. Guyan, "Mittelalterlichen Wüstlegungen." See also Fuhrmann, *Germany in the High Middle Ages*, esp. 6–30.

12. German has a new term, for wetlands dried up by river channel-ization: **versteppung**. See Blackbourn, *Conquest of Nature*, 12.

13. See Lamb, *Historic Storms of the North Sea* for an introduction to period storms.

14. Buisman, *Duizend jaar weer, wind en water*, vol. 1, offers a detailed analysis.

15. Van der Stadt, *Nederland in zeven overstromingen*.

16. At the end of the eighteenth century the situation remained grim in some spots: see Bachiene, *Vaderlandsche geographie*, 3:1159–1386.

17. On Dunwich, see Comfort, *Lost City*, and Manning, *Dunwich*.

18. Carter, *Forgotten Ports*, 23–38.

19. Jakubowski-Tiessen, *Sturmflut 1717* is a detailed history of this less serious but still culture-wrenching storm.

20. In Heine, *North Sea*, 70–71.

21. Much of Tolkien's work is grounded in sophisticated under-standing of folkore; see, for example, Davidson, "Folklore and Man's Past," and Opie, "Tentacles of Tradition." On the folklore of houses especially, see William, "Protection of the House."

22. Laslett, *World We Have Lost*, 80. See also Chisholm, *Rural Settlement*, 48–50. Walking speed governs much spacing in traditional landscape.

23. On early bicycles in villages, see Moreau, *Departed Village*, 132–142.

24. Beresford, *History on the Ground*, 96–97.

25. Mowat, *West Viking*, emphasizes what individuals may learn from direct observation in Newfoundland: see esp. 314–319.

26. Fagan, *The Little Ice Age* is a good introduction. For a more detailed study, see Grove, *Little Ice Age*.

27. Mckinzey, Ólafsdóttir, and Dugmore, "Perception, History, and Science" offers an introduction to such in Iceland.

28. See Ruddock, "Columbus and Iceland," and Quinn, "Columbus and the North." The Inuit differ from the extinct Dorset, whose ruins the Norse found: the Dorset may have been unable to survive in the warm centuries preceding the Norse arrival.

29. On climate change and its effects in the period, see Lamb, *Climate: Present, Past, Future* and *Climate, History, and the Modern World*.

30. Stilgoe, *Common Landscape*, esp. 135–202. See also Pastore, *Between Land and Sea*.

31. Stilgoe, *Borderland*, provides one view of the importance of the stead in American concepts of suburban landscape.

6 FARM

1. Stilgoe, *Borderland*, esp. 67–127.

2. Shipley, *Dictionary*, explicates the argument for the Latin origin of the modern English word **farm**.

3. See also Cooper, *Farm*, and Elliott, *On the Farm*.

4. Plunkett, *Rural Life* pioneered an entire genre.

5. Black, *Law Dictionary*, under "pascua."

6. Shakespeare, *As You Like It*, II.i.

7. Turner, *First and Second Partes*, I, B, viii. The true marshmallow is not the common mallow.

8. Ponge, *Making of the Pré*, 57.

9. Darby, *Domesday England* is a good introduction.

10. See Williams, ed., *Domesday Book* for background.

11. Lennard, *Rural England* remains a strong introduction to such details.

12. Stilgoe, *Landscape and Images*, 47–63.

13. "Grip" still designates intestinal flu.

14. Galfridus, *Promptorium parvulorum*, 213.

15. Atwell, *Faithful Surveyor*, 91.

16. Hardy, "In Time of 'The Breaking of Nations,'" in *Selected Poems*, 203.

7 WAYS

1. Collected in the early 1840s and translated into English about 1852, the Norwegian tale, now sanitized, is brutally violent: see Asbjørnsen and Moe, *Popular Tales*, 264–266.

2. Since 1987 three kindergarten teachers have remarked on this.

3. Watching little children approach wood footbridges in conservation areas proves instructive. Experiments involving lurking beneath such bridges and growling and hissing prove more so.

4. Murtha, *Bobbie Gentry's "Ode to Billie Joe,"* xii–9.

5. Margary, *Roman Roads in Britain* makes clear the importance of imperial highways and garrisons.

6. Pierce, *Old London Bridge* is a good introduction to the site and the inhabited bridge.

7. Hentzner, *Journey into England*, 14.

8. Of course they connote much more beyond the scope of this book: see Bachelard, *L'eau et les rêves*.

9. Matthew 11:28. Contemporary biblical translation "modernizes" terminology and deprives young people of Sunday morning etymological stretching.

10. Rae, *Road and the Car* introduces this issue in nuanced ways.

11. Wynne, *Growing Up Suburban*, 134–169 and passim.

12. On land measurement and surveying see Richeson, *English Land Measuring*.

13. Rothfuss, *Name of the Wind* offers an excellent illustration: see esp. 1–53.

14. Ray, *Collection*, under "bree": iv–vi. See also Gladstone, "'New World of English Words.'"

15. Stilgoe, *Common Landscape*, 21, 53.

16. Abandoned landscape figures in glamour and other types of power: see Stilgoe, *Old Fields*.

17. Tolkien, *Lord of the Rings*, 1:187–286, esp. 206–208, 253, 270–273: for the quotation, see 280.

18. See, for example, Cooper, *Dark Is Rising*. The role of quality fantasy fiction in shaping landscape concepts among bright young readers rewards any amount of attention.

19. See, for example, Farren, *Texts of Festival*, which emphasizes the great swamps that reappeared around London.

20. Lee, *Lord of the Rings Sketchbook*, 24; see also 33.

21. Howe, *Fantasy Art Workshop*, 80.

22. When offered the opportunity, undergraduates write superbly about the significance of Tolkien's books, often emphasizing how landscape endures in their understanding of his books and in the world around them.

23. On the paradigm shift, see Raisz, *Atlas of Global Geography*.

24. Platt, *English Medieval Town* offers an excellent introduction.

25. It is not in Johnson's *Dictionary*, for example.

26. Eliade, *Sacred and the Profane*, 46–67.

27. See Daniel, *Bible in English*, and Cummings, *Book of Common Prayer*, for an introduction. Both the Bible and the *Book of Common Prayer* shaped Shakespeare.

28. Hannan, *Inventing Freedom* provides a thought-provoking introduction to the connections.

29. Biedermann, *Dictionary of Symbolism*, 35–40; see also Lancre, *Tableau*.

8 FIELD

1. Shakespeare, *Midsummer Night's Dream*, II.i.

2. Bacon, *Sylva Sylvarum*, §228.

3. See, for example, Weber, *Handwörterbuch der deutschen Sprache* (1892), under "landschaft," and Weigand, *Deutsches Wörterbuch* (1910), under "land." Weigand does not mention "landschaft."

4. One dense, alternative view of German thinking can be found in *Deutsche Landschaft*, edited by Helmut J. Schneider: it rarely mentions geographers.

5. Most mariners used British Admiralty charts, one way Britain ruled the seas.

6. *Meyers geographischer Hand-Atlas* (1905) demonstrates the remapping well.

7. Wood and Fels provide a superb view of maps as fields of concepts in *The Natures of Maps*, esp. 6–17. See also Black, *Maps and History: Constructing Images of the Past*. Recently, for example, the United States federal government changed the name of the Persian Gulf to the **Arabian Gulf**.

8. On house-building, for example, see Bächtold-Stäubli, *Handwörterbuch*, 1557–1567.

9. See the definitions of "land," "landschaft," and related words (especially **landkarte** [on mapping]) in *Der Grosse Brockhaus*, 11, 65–112, for a succinct overview of early 1930s German viewpoints, and Breul, *Heath's German and English Dictionary* (1906), under "landschaft," for an example of the political basis of the term. The *Chambers Dictionary of Etymology* hints at issues the *OED* ignores: see under "landscape." See also Heinsius, *Nederlandsche taal*, under **landschop**.

10. Given contemporaneous connotations of "region," at least in the United States, his effort seems futile in retrospect.

11. Olwig, "Rediscovering the Substantive Nature of Landscape" is especially acute.

12. Hartshorne, *Nature of Geography*, 149–153, 159–160, 163–165.

13. Grafton, *Chronicle*, 2:84.

14. Manguel, *A Reader on Reading*, notes the difficulties of translating into English the several German words denoting value. "Landscape" perhaps follows a similar pattern: see 254–263.

15. See Olwig, "Recovering the Substantive Nature of Landscape"; Austin, "The Castle and the Landscape"; Coones, "One Landscape or Many?"; and Muir, "Conceptualizing Landscape."

16. Maxwell, *Detective in Kent*, 114.

17. Ibid., 135.

18. Ibid., 54.

19. Ibid., 108–109. For other inquiries influenced by Maxwell, see for example Rippon, "Focus or Frontier?"; Parker, "Maritime Landscapes"; and Murphy, "Submerged Prehistoric Landscapes."

20. Tennyson understood harmony: see *Suffolk Scene*, esp. 4–5. He died in World War II. See also Carter, *Forgotten Ports*.

21. On the television series, see Taylor, "*The Making of the English Landscape* and Beyond."

22. On Jackson's understanding of time, see especially his *A Sense of Place, a Sense of Time*.

9 AWAY

1. Manguel, *City of Words*, 76.

2. Milgram, "Experience of Living in Cities," esp. 1464–1466, proves a useful caution.

3. Olmsted, "Disuse of Older Landscape Words," 15–16.

BIBLIOGRAPHY

Abbey, Edward. *Desert Solitaire: A Season in the Wilderness.* New York: McGraw-Hill, 1968.

Abel, Wilhem. *Die Wüstungen des ausgehenden Mittelalters.* Stuttgart: Gustav Fischer, 1955.

Acciavatti, Anthony. *Ganges Water Machine: Designing New India's Ancient River.* San Francisco: Applied Research and Design Publishing, 2015.

Admiralty. *Manual of Seamanship.* 2 vols. London: His Majesty's Stationery Office, 1908.

Aitchison, Jean. *Words in the Mind: An Introduction to the Mental Lexicon.* [1987.] 4th ed. London: Wiley-Blackwell, 2012.

Andrew, Laurence. *The Noble Lyfe and Natures of Bestes.* Antwerp: Iohn of Doesborowe, 1527.

Ansted, A. *A Dictionary of Sea Terms.* Glasgow: Crown, 1920.

Asbjørnsen, Peter Christian, and Jörgen Moe. *Popular Tales from the North.* [1841.] Trans. George W. Dasent. Edinburgh: David Douglas, 1912.

Atwell, George. *The Faithful Surveyor.* London: Needham, 1665.

Austin: David. "The Castle and the Landscape." *Landscape History* 6 (1984): 69–81.

Bachelard, Gaston. *L'eau et les rêves: Essai sur l'imagination de la matière.* Paris: José Corti, 1942.

Bachelard, Gaston. *The Psychoanalysis of Fire.* [1938.] Trans. Alan C. M. Ross. Boston: Beacon Press, 1964.

Bachiene, Willem Albert. *Vaderlandsche geographie, of Nieuwe tegenwoordige Staat en hedendaagsche historie der Nederlanden.* 5 vols. Amsterdam: Gartman, Vermandel, Smit, 1791.

Bächtold-Stäubli, Hanns. *Handwörterbuch des deutschen Aberglaubens.* 10 vols. Berlin: de Gruyter, 1927–1942.

Bacon, Francis. *Sylva Sylvarum: or, A Natural History in Ten Centuries.* London: W. Lee, 1626.

Barnes, Roger. *The Dinghy Cruising Companion: Tales and Advice from Sailing in a Small Open Boat.* London: Adlard Coles, 2014.

Bartlett, John Russell. *Dictionary of Americanisms: A Glossary of Words and Phrases Usually Regarded as Peculiar to the United States.* [1848.] Boston: Little, Brown, 1859.

Béjoint, Henri. *The Lexicography of English.* Oxford: Oxford University Press, 2010.

Bellenden, John. *Livy's History of Rome.* [1533.] Edinburgh: Tait, 1822.

Beresford, Maurice. *History on the Ground: Six Studies in Maps and Landscapes.* [1957.] Rev. ed. London: Methuen, 1971.

Beresford, Maurice. *The Lost Villages of England.* London: Lutterworth, 1954.

Beresford, Maurice. *Lost Villages of Yorkshire.* Leeds: Yorkshire Archaeological Society, 1951.

Beresford, Maurice. *Wharram Percy: Deserted Medieval Village.* London: Batsford, 1990.

Berlin, Leslie. "Robert Noyce, Silicon Valley, and the Teamwork behind the High-Technology Revolution." *Magazine of History* 24 (January 2010): 33–36.

Biedermann, Hans. *Dictionary of Symbolism: Cultural Icons and the Meanings behind Them.* New York: Meridian, 1994.

Black, Henry Campbell. *Black's Law Dictionary.* [1891.] Rev. ed. St. Paul, MN: West, 1933.

Black, Jeremy. *Maps and History: Constructing Images of the Past.* New Haven: Yale University Press, 1997.

Blackbourn, David. *The Conquest of Nature: Water, Landscape, and the Making of Modern Germany.* New York: Norton, 2006.

Blackstone, William. *Commentaries on the Laws of England.* 4 vols. Dublin: Exshaw, 1770.

Boileau, D., and A. Picquot. *A New Dictionary in French and English.* London: Longman, 1839.

Boissonnade, P. *Life and Work in Medieval Europe: The Evolution of Medieval Economy from the Fifth to the Fifteenth Century.* [1927.] Trans. Eileen Power. New York: Harper and Row, 1964.

Bonforte, Lisa. *Who Lives on the Farm?* New York: Golden, 1980.

Bothwell, J. S., ed. *The Age of Edward III.* Woodbridge, UK: York Medieval Press, 2001.

Boyd-Bowman, Peter. *From Latin to Romance in Sound Charts.* Washington, DC: Georgetown University Press, 1980.

Boyd-Bowman, Peter. *Léxico hispanoamericano del siglo XVI.* [1971.] Madison, WI: Hispanic Seminary, 1982.

Boyd-Bowman, Peter. "Regional Origins of the Earliest Spanish Colonists of America." *Publications of the Modern Language Association* 71 (December 1956): 1152–1162.

Boyer, Abel. *Royal Dictionary.* [1699.] Ed. N. Salmon. London: Rivington, 1819.

Brace, Gerald Warner. *Between Wind and Water*. New York: Norton, 1966.

Bradford, Ernle. *Mediterranean: Portrait of a Sea*. New York: Harcourt, 1971.

Breul, Karl. *Heath's German and English Dictionary*. Boston: Heath, 1906.

Brooks, Charles E. P. *Climate through the Ages: A Study of the Climatic Factors and Their Variation*. [1926.] Rev. ed. London: Ernest Benn, 1949.

Brown, Christopher. *Dutch Landscape: The Early Years, Haarlem and Amsterdam, 1590–1650*. London: National Gallery, 1986.

Brown, Kevin V. "How You Can Own and Fly Your Own Whirlybird." *Popular Science* 176 (July 1970): 41–43, 105, 107.

Brown, Vinson. *Reading the Outdoors at Night*. Mechanicsburg, PA: Stackpole, 1982.

Brucker, Herbert. "The Airplane and the Average Man." *Review of Reviews* 80 (July 1929): 54–61.

Brusatin, Manlio. *A History of Colors*. [1983.] Trans. Robert H. Hopcke and Paul Schwarz. Boston: Shambhala, 1991.

Buisman, Jan. *Duizend jaar weer, wind, en water in de Lage Landen*. 5 vols. Franeker, Netherlands: Van Wijner, 1995.

Burke, Peter. *Popular Culture in Early Modern Europe*. New York: Harper, 1978.

Butcher, David. *Lowestoft, 1550–1750: Development and Change in a Suffolk Coastal Town*. Woodbridge, UK: Boydell, 2008.

Carter, George Goldsmith. *Forgotten Ports of England*. London: Evans Brothers, 1951.

Cassidy, Frederic G., et al. *Dictionary of American Regional English*. 5 vols. Cambridge, MA: Harvard University Press, 1985–2012.

Casson, Herbert N. *The Priceless Art of Observation*. London: Efficiency Magazine, 1936.

Century Dictionary: An Encyclopedic Lexicon of the English Language. 12 vols. New York: Century, 1914.

Chamberlin, Clarence D. "Shall We Let Our Children Fly?" *Parents' Magazine* 5 (January 1930): 14–19.

Chambers Dictionary of Etymology. Edinburgh: Chambers Harrap, 1988.

Charles, Prince of Wales. *Harmony: A New Way of Looking at Our World.* New York: HarperCollins, 2010.

Charnock, Richard Stephen. *Local Etymology: A Derivative Dictionary of Geographical Names.* London: Houlston and Wright, 1859.

Chiles, James R. "Flying Cars Were a Dream that Never Got Off the Ground." *Smithsonian Magazine* 27 (February 1989): 144–162.

Chisholm, Michael. *Rural Settlement and Land Use: An Essay in Location.* London: Hutchinson, 1962.

Clapin, Sylva. *Dictionnaire canadien-français.* Montreal: Beauchemin, 1894.

Clapin, Sylva. *A New Dictionary of Americanisms.* New York: Weiss, 1902.

Clark, Kenneth. *Landscape into Art.* London: John Murray, 1949.

Clarke, D. H. *East Coast Passage: The Voyage of a Thames Sailing Barge.* London: Longman, 1971.

Coke, Edward. *The First Part of the Institutes of the Laws of England.* London: Richard More, 1629.

Comfort, Nicholas A. *The Lost City of Dunwich.* Lavenham, UK: Terence Dalton, 1994.

Coombs, F. Lovell. "Young Crusoes of the Sky." *St. Nicholas* 38 (April 1911): 516–523.

Coones, Paul. "One Landscape or Many? A Geographical Perspective." *Landscape History* 7 (1985): 5–12.

Cooper, Elisha. *Farm*. New York: Orchard, 2010.

Cooper, James Fenimore. *The Bee-hunter; or, The Oak Openings*. London: Bentley, 1848.

Cooper, Susan. *The Dark Is Rising*. New York: Simon and Schuster, 1973.

Cornish, Vaughan. *The Beauties of Scenery: A Geographical Survey*. London: Muller, 1943.

Cornish, Vaughan. *Ocean Waves and Kindred Geophysical Phenomena*. Cambridge: Cambridge University Press, 1934.

Cornish, Vaughan. *Scenery and the Sense of Sight*. Cambridge: Cambridge University Press, 1935.

Cornish, Vaughan. *The Scenery of England: A Study of Harmonious Grouping in Town and Country*. London: Council for the Preservation of Rural England, 1932.

Cotgrave, Randle. *A Dictionarie of the French and English Tongues*. London: Adam Islip, 1611.

Cottrell, Mark. *Kite Aerial Photography*. London: Kite Store, 1987.

Cronon, William. *Changes in the Land: Indians, Colonists, and the Ecology of New England*. New York: Hill and Wang, 1983.

Crouch, Nathaniel. *The English Empire in America*. 4 vols. London: Crouch, 1698.

Cuban, Larry. *How Teachers Taught: Constancy and Change in American Classrooms*. New York: Teachers College Press, 1993.

Cummings, Brian, ed. *The Book of Common Prayer: The Texts of 1549, 1559, and 1662*. Oxford: Oxford University Press, 2011.

Daniel, David. *The Bible in English: Its History and Influence*. New Haven: Yale University Press, 2003.

Darby, Henry C. *Domesday England*. Cambridge: Cambridge University Press, 1959.

Davidson, H. R. Ellis. "Folklore and Man's Past." *Folklore* 74 (Winter 1963): 527–544.

De Beauffort, G., and M. Dusariez. *Aerial Photographs Taken from Kites: Yesterday and Today*. Pitman, NJ: Kapwa Foundation Publishing, 1995.

Defoe, Daniel. *The Life and Strange Adventures of Robinson Crusoe*. [1719.] Ed. G. H. Maynadier. 3 vols. Boston: Old Corner, 1903.

De Garis, Marie. *Dictionnaire anglais-guernésiais*. Chichester, Sussex: Phillimore, 1982.

De la Grasserie, Raoul. *Des parlers des différentes classes sociales*. Paris: Geuthner, 1909.

De Lancre, Pierre. *Tableau de l'inconstance des mauvais anges et démons*. Paris: Berjon, 1612.

Delderfield, R. F. *A Horseman Riding By*. New York: Simon and Schuster, 1967.

De Vere, Schele. *Americanisms: The English of the New World*. New York: Scribner, 1872.

De Vries, Jan, and F. de Tollenaere. *Etymologisch woordenboek*. Utrecht: Spectrum, 2002.

De Vries, Jan, and F. de Tollenaere. *Nederlands etymologisch woordenboek*. Leiden: Brill, 1971.

Dickson, D. Bruce. *The Dawn of Belief: Religion in the Upper Paleolithic of Southwestern Europe*. Tucson: University of Arizona Press, 1990.

Dictionary of American Regional English. 5 vols. Cambridge, MA: Harvard University Press, 1985–2012.

Dictionnaire de l'Académie Française. 3 vols. Paris: Didot, 1835.

Dictionnaire universel françois et latin. 5 vols. Paris: Delaune, 1732.

Dietze, Gottfried. *Magna Carta and Property.* Charlottesville: University of Virginia Press, 1965.

Doornkaat Koolman, J. ten. *Wörterbuch der ostfriesischen Sprache.* 3 vols. Norden, Germany: Herman Braams, 1882.

Downes, P. G. *Sleeping Island.* New York: Coward-McCann, 1943.

"Dragon-fly." *Scribner's Magazine* 58 (July 1915): 105.

Dugdale, William. *The History of Imbanking and Drayning of Divers Fennes and Marshes Both in Foreign Parts and in this Kingdom and of the Improvements Thereby.* London: Alice Warren, 1662.

Duryea, Charles E. "The Universal Road." *Good Roads* 3 (July 1894): 23–27.

Dye, Margaret. *Dinghy Cruising: The Enjoyment of Wandering Afloat.* [1992.] London: Adlard Coles, 2006.

Eckener, Hugo. *Die Amerikafahrt des "Graf Zeppelin."* Berlin: Scherl, 1928.

Eddy, William A. "Photographing from Kites." *Century Magazine* 54 (May 1897): 86–91.

Eliade, Mircea. *The Sacred and the Profane: The Nature of Religion.* New York: Harcourt, Brace, 1959.

Elliott, David. *On the Farm.* Cambridge, MA: Candlewick, 2008.

Eyges, Leonard. *The Practical Pilot: Coastal Navigation by Eye, Intuition, and Common Sense.* Camden, ME: International Marine, 1989.

Fagan, Brian M. *The Little Ice Age: How Climate Made History, 1300–1500.* New York: Basic, 2000.

Falconer, William. *An Universal Dictionary of the Marine.* [1769.] London: Cadell, 1780.

Farren, Mick. *The Texts of Festival.* New York: Avon, 1973.

Fitter, Chris. *Poetry, Space, Landscape: Toward a New Theory.* Cambridge: Cambridge University Press, 1995.

Freeman-Grenville, G. S. P., ed. *The East African Coast: Select Documents from the First to the Earlier Nineteenth Century.* Oxford: Clarendon Press, 1962.

Friend, Joseph Harold. *The Development of American Lexicography, 1798–1864.* The Hague: Mouton, 1967.

Fuhrmann, Horst. *Germany in the High Middle Ages, c. 1050–1200.* Trans. Timothy Reuter. Cambridge: Cambridge University Press, 1986.

Galfridus, Anglicus. *Promptorium parvulorum sive clericorum, lexicon Anglo-Latinum princeps.* [c. 1470.] London: Camden Society, 1843.

Gamble, Clive. *Timewalkers: The Prehistory of Global Colonization.* Cambridge, MA: Harvard University Press, 1994.

Gentry, Bobbie. *Ode to Billie Joe.* New York: Universal Music Publishing Group, 1967.

Gladstone, Jo. "'New World of English Words': John Ray, FRS, the Dialect Protagonist in the Context of his Times (1658–1691)." In Peter Burke and Roy Porter, eds., *Language, Self, and Society: A Social History of Language,* 115–153. Cambridge, MA: Polity, 1991.

Goethe, Johann Wolfgang von. *Italian Journey.* Ed. Thomas P. Saine and Jeffrey L. Sammons. Princeton, NJ: Princeton University Press, 1989.

Grafton, Richard. *A Chronicle at Large and Meere History of the Affayres of Englande.* [1568.] 3 vols. London: Johnson, 1809.

Grahame, Kenneth. *The Wind in the Willows.* London: Methuen, 1908.

Graves, Robert. *Selected Poems.* Ed. Paul O'Prey. New York: Penguin, 1986.

Greenwood, Paul. *Once aboard a Cornish Lugger.* Clifton-upon-Teme, Worcestershire: Polperro Heritage Press, 2007.

Grimm, Jacob, and Wilhelm Grimm. *The Annotated Brothers Grimm.* Ed. and trans. Maria Tatar. New York: Norton, 2012.

Grinsell, Leslie. "The Christianisation of Prehistoric and Other Pagan Sites." *Landscape History* 8 (1986): 27–37.

Groot woordenboek der Nederlandse taal. 5 vols. Utrecht: Dale, 1992.

Grose, Francis. *Classical Dictionary of the Vulgar Tongue.* London: Hooper, 1785.

Der Grosse Brockhaus. Leipzig: Brockhaus, 1932.

Grove, Jean M. *The Little Ice Age.* London: Routledge, 1990.

Guldi, Joanna. *Roads to Power: Britain Invents the Infrastructure State.* Cambridge, MA: Harvard University Press, 2012.

Guyan, Walter Ulrich. "Die mittelalterlichen Wüstlegungen als archäologisches und geographisches Problem dargelegt an einigen Beispielen aus dem Kanton Schaffhausen." *Zeitschrift für Schweizerische Geschichte* 26 (1946): 433–478.

Häberle, Daniel. *Die Wüstungen der Rheinpfalz, Beiträge zur Landeskunde der Rheinpfalz.* Kaiserslautern, Germany: n.p., 1922.

Halliwell, James Orchard. *Dictionary of Archaic and Provincial Words.* 2 vols. London: John Russell Smith, 1847.

Halliwell, James Orchard. *Rambles in Western Cornwall.* London: John Russell Smith, 1861.

Hannan, Daniel. *Inventing Freedom: How the English-Speaking Peoples Made the Modern World.* New York: HarperCollins, 2013.

Hardy, Thomas. "In Time of 'The Breaking of Nations.'" In *Selected Poems.* London: Macmillan, 1916.

Hartshorne, Richard. *The Nature of Geography: A Critical Survey of Current Thought in the Light of the Past.* Lancaster, PA: Association of American Geographers, 1939.

Hawes, Louis. *Presences of Nature: British Landscape, 1780–1830.* New Haven: Yale Center for British Art, 1982.

Heine, Heinrich. "A Wraith in the Sea." In *The North Sea*. [1825.] Trans. Howard Mumford Jones. Chicago: Open Court, 1916.

Heinsius, J. *Nederlandsche taal*. 4 vols. Leiden: Nijhoff, 1916.

Hentzner, Paul. *A Journey into England*. [1598.] Edinburgh: Aungervyle Society, 1881.

Hinchman, Hannah. *A Trail through Leaves: The Journal as a Path to Place*. New York: Norton, 1997.

Hoffman, Donald D. *Visual Intelligence: How We Create What We See*. New York: Norton, 1998.

Holme, C. G. "The Influence of the Air." *Creative Art* 5 (October 1929): 725–728.

Hoskins, W. G. *English Landscapes*. London: British Broadcasting Corporation, 1973.

Hoskins, W. G. *The Making of the English Landscape*. London: Hodder and Stoughton, 1955.

Hoskins, W. G. *Old Devon*. London: David and Charles, 1966.

Hoskins, W. G. *One Man's England*. London: British Broadcasting Corporation, 1978.

Howard, A. E. Dick. *Magna Carta*. Charlottesville: University of Virginia Press, 1998.

Howe, John. *Fantasy Art Workshop*. London: David and Charles, 2007.

Howell, James. *Lexicon Tetraglotton: English-French-Italian-Spanish Dictionary*. London: C. Bee, 1660.

Howse, Derek, and Norman J. W. Thrower, eds. *A Buccaneer's Atlas: Basil Ringrose's South Sea Waggoner: A Sea Atlas and Sailing Directions of the Pacific Coast of the Americas, 1682*. Berkeley: University of California Press, 1992.

Hugo, Victor. *The Toilers of the Sea*. [1866.] New York: Burt, 1888.

Hugo, Victor. *The Toilers of the Sea*. [1866]. Ed. Graham Robb, trans. James Hogarth. New York: Random House, 1992.

Hüllen, Werner. *English Dictionaries 800–1700: The Topical Tradition*. Oxford: Oxford University Press, 1999.

Irving, Washington. *A Tour of the Prairies*. New York: Belford, 1800.

Jackson, J. B. *American Space: The Centennial Years, 1865–1876*. New York: Norton, 1972.

Jackson, J. B. *Discovering the Vernacular Landscape*. New Haven: Yale University Press, 1984.

Jackson. J. B. "Ghosts at the Door." *Landscape* 1 (Autumn 1951): 3–9. Reprinted in Ervin H. Zube and Margaret J. Zube, eds., *Changing Rural Landscapes* (Amherst: University of Massachusetts Press, 1977).

Jackson, J. B. *Landscapes*. Ed. Ervin H. Zube. Amherst: University of Massachusetts Press, 1970.

Jackson, J. B. *The Necessity for Ruins and Other Topics*. Amherst: University of Massachusetts Press, 1980.

Jackson, J. B. "New Fields." *Art and Architecture* 1 (1956): n.p.

Jackson, J. B. *A Sense of Place, a Sense of Time*. New Haven: Yale University Press, 1994.

Jakubowski-Tiessen, Manfred. *Sturmflut 1717: Die Bewältigung einer Naturkatastrophe in der Frühen Neuzeit*. Munich: Oldenbourg, 1992.

Jewett, Sarah Orne. *The Country of the Pointed Firs*. Boston: Houghton Mifflin, 1896.

Johnson, Samuel. *A Dictionary of the English Language*. 2 vols. London: Knapton, 1755.

Jones, Howard Mumford. *Howard Mumford Jones: An Autobiography*. Madison: University of Wisconsin Press, 1979.

Jones, Mari C. *Jersey Norman French: A Linguistic Study of an Obsolescent Dialect*. Oxford, UK: Philological Society, 2001.

Jones, Stephen. *Short Voyages*. New York: Norton, 1985.

Jones, Stephen. *Working Thin Waters: Conversations with Captain Lawrence H. Malloy, Jr.* Hanover, NH: University Press of New England, 2001.

Jones, Tristan. *A Steady Trade: A Boyhood at Sea*. London: Bodley Head, 1982.

Kaplan, Robert D. *The Coming Anarchy: Shattering the Dreams of the Post Cold War*. New York: Random House, 2000.

Karlsson, Elis. *Mother Sea*. London: Oxford University Press, 1964.

Karlsson, Elis. *Pully-Haul: The Story of a Voyage*. London: Oxford University Press, 1966.

Kennedy, Peter. *La Collection Jersiaise: Folk Music, Customs, and Speech*. London: Folktracks Cassettes, 1977.

Kersey, John. *A New English Dictionary*. London: Henry Bonwick, 1702.

King, Dean. *A Sea of Words: A Lexicon and Companion for Patrick O'Brian's Seafaring Tales*. New York: Holt, 1995.

Kurath, Hans. *Linguistic Atlas of New England*. 6 vols. Providence: Brown University Press, 1939–1943.

Lamb, H. H. *Climate, History, and the Modern World*. [1982.] Rev. ed. London: Routledge, 1995.

Lamb, H. H. *Climate: Present, Past, Future*. 2 vols. London: Methuen, 1973–1975.

Lamb, H. H. *Historic Storms of the North Sea, British Isles, and Northwest Europe*. Cambridge: Cambridge University Press, 1991.

Landrum, Carl A. *Historical Sketches of Quincy, Illinois*. Quincy, IL: Historical Society, 1986.

Langewiesche, Wolfgang. *I'll Take the High Road*. New York: Harcourt, Brace, 1939.

Laslett, Peter. *The World We Have Lost: England before the Industrial Age*. [1965.] New York: Scribner's, 1971.

Lee, Alan. *The Lord of the Rings Sketchbook*. Boston: Houghton Mifflin, 2005.

Le Guin, Ursula K. *A Wizard of Earthsea*. Berkeley, CA: Parnassus, 1968.

Lennard, Reginald. *Rural England 1086–1135: A Study of Social and Agrarian Conditions*. Oxford: Oxford University Press, 1959.

Lent, Henry B. *Clear Track Ahead*. New York: Macmillan, 1937.

Lindbergh, Anne Morrow. "Airliner to Europe: Notes from a Passenger's Diary." *Harper's Magazine* 197 (September 1948): 42–47.

Lindbergh, Anne Morrow. *Gift from the Sea*. New York: Pantheon, 1955.

Lindbergh, Anne Morrow. *North to the Orient*. New York: Harcourt, 1935.

Lindbergh, Charles A. *We*. New York: Putnam's, 1927.

Linn, John Blair. *History of Centre and Clinton Counties*. Philadelphia: Everts, 1883.

Liszka, Thomas R., and Lorna E. M. Walker. *The North Sea World in the Middle Ages: Studies in the Cultural History of North-Western Europe*. Dublin: Four Courts Press, 2001.

Littleton, Thomas. *Tenures*. London: Iohanes Willes, 1482.

Lukis, Eric Fellowes. *An Outline of the Franco-Norman Dialect of Guernsey*. Guernsey: Europrint, 1981.

Maillet, Antonine. *Rabelais et les traditions populaires en Acadie*. Laval, Quebec: Presses de l'Université Laval, 1971.

Mak, Geert. *An Island in Time: The Biography of a Village.* [1988.] Trans. Ann Kelland. London: Vintage, 2010.

Manguel, Alberto. *The City of Words.* Toronto: Anansi, 2007.

Manguel, Alberto. *The Library at Night.* New Haven: Yale University Press, 2006.

Manguel, Alberto. *A Reader on Reading.* New Haven: Yale University Press, 2010.

Manning, A. S. *Dunwich: East Anglia's Atlantis.* Ilfracombe, UK: Stockwell, 1995.

Margary, Ivan D. *Roman Roads in Britain.* London: Phoenix, 1955.

Markham, Beryl. *West with the Night.* Cambridge, MA: Houghton Mifflin, 1942.

Mawson, C. O. Sylvester, ed. *The New Thesaurus of English Words and Phrases Classified and Arranged so as to Facilitate the Expression of Ideas and Assist in Literary Composition, Based on the Classic Work of P. M. Roget.* New York: Current Literature, 1911.

Maxwell, Donald. *A Detective in Kent: Landscape Clues to the Discovery of Lost Seas.* London: John Lane, 1929.

Mayhew, Robert J. *Landscape, Literature and English Religious Culture, 1660–1800: Samuel Johnson and Languages of Natural Description.* London: Palgrave, 2004.

McGowan, Susan, and Amelia F. Miller. *Family and Landscape: Deerfield Homelots from 1671.* Deerfield, MA: Pocumtuck Valley Memorial Association, 1996.

Mckinzey, Krista M., Rannveig Ólafsdóttir, and Andrew J. Dugmore. "Perception, History, and Science: Coherence or Disparity in the Timing of the Little Ice Age Maximum in Southeast Iceland?" *Polar Record* 41 (Fall 2005): 319–334.

Melbin, Murray. "Night as Frontier." *American Sociological Journal* 43 (Spring 1978): 3–22.

Mellor, John. *The Art of Pilotage*. Dobbs Ferry, NY: Sheridan House, 1990.

Meyers geographischer Hand-Atlas. Leipzig: Bibliographisches Institut, 1905.

Milan, William, ed. *1974 Colloquium on Spanish and Portuguese Linguistics*. Washington, DC: Georgetown University Press, 1975.

Milgram, Stanley. "The Experience of Living in Cities." *Science* 97 (March 13, 1970): 1461–1468.

Milton, John. *Poetical Works*. Ed. H. C. Beeching. London: Oxford University Press, 1938.

Minnaert, M. G. J. *Light and Color in the Outdoors*. [1937.] Trans. Len Seymour. Rev. ed. New York: Springer, 1993.

Mitchell, Donald G. *Reveries of a Bachelor*. New York: Scribner, 1863.

Moore, Ruth. *Candlemas Bay*. New York: Morrow, 1950.

Morand, Paul. *Air indien*. Paris: Bernard Grasset, 1932.

Moreau, R. E. *The Departed Village: Berrick Salome at the Turn of the Century*. London: Oxford University Press, 1968.

Morgan, Willard D., and Henry M. Lester. *Graphic Graflex Photography: The Master Book for the Larger Camera*. [1940.] New York: Morgan and Lester, 1948.

Mowat, Farley. *West Viking: The Ancient Norse in Greenland and North America*. Toronto: McClelland and Steward, 1965.

Muir, Richard. "Conceptualizing Landscape." *Landscapes* 1 (2000): 4–21.

Muir, Richard. *Landscape Detective: Discovering a Countryside*. Macclesfield, UK: Windgather, 2001.

Mulville, Frank. *Terschelling Sands*. London: Conway Maritime, 1968.

Murphy, Peter. "The Submerged Prehistoric Landscapes of the Southern North Sea: Work in Progress." *Landscapes* 1 (2007): 1–22.

Murtha, Tara. *Bobbie Gentry's "Ode to Billie Joe."* New York: Bloomsbury, 2015.

Musson, Anthony. *Medieval Law in Context: The Growth of Legal Consciousness from Magna Carta to the Peasants' Revolt.* Manchester: Manchester University Press, 2001.

Neev, David, and K. O. Emery. *The Destruction of Sodom, Gomorrah, and Jericho: Geological, Climatological, and Archaeological Background.* Oxford: Oxford University Press, 1995.

Newton, Arthur Percival. *The Great Age of Discovery.* London: University of London Press, 1932.

Nicholls, C. S. *The Swahili Coast: Politics, Diplomacy and Trade on the East African Littoral, 1798–1856.* London: Allen and Unwin, 1971.

O'Brien, Conor. *Sea-Boats, Oars, and Sails.* London: Oxford University Press, 1941.

Oliphant, B. J. *Death Served Up Cold.* New York: Fawcett, 1994.

Oliver, Kev, and Tony Lancashire. *Blokes Up North: Through the Heart of the Northwest Passage by Sail and Oar.* London: Lodestar, 2014.

Olmsted, Frederick Law. "The Disuse of Older Landscape Words and Terms." *Landscape Architecture* 11 (October 1920): 13–18.

Olwig, Kenneth R. "Recovering the Substantive Nature of Landscape." *Annals of the Association of American Geographers* 86 (December 1996): 630–653.

Onions, C. T., ed. *The Oxford Dictionary of English Etymology.* Oxford: Oxford University Press, 1966.

Opie, Peter. "The Tentacles of Tradition." *Folklore* 73 (Winter 1963): 507–526.

The Oxford English Dictionary. 2nd ed. 20 vols. Oxford: Oxford University Press, 1991.

Park, Chris. *A Dictionary of Environment and Conservation.* Oxford: Oxford University Press, 2007.

Parker, A. J. "Maritime Landscapes." *Landscapes* 1 (2007): 22–41.

Partridge, Eric. *A Dictionary of the Underworld: British and American.* London: Theodore Brun, 1950.

Partridge, Eric. *Origins: A Short Etymological Dictionary of Modern English.* New York: Macmillan, 1959.

Pastore, Christopher L. *Between Land and Sea: The Atlantic Coast and the Transformation of New England.* Cambridge, MA: Harvard University Press, 2014.

Petersham, Maud, and Miska Petersham. *The Story Book of Trains.* Chicago: Winston, 1935.

Pierce, Patricia. *Old London Bridge: The Story of the Largest Inhabited Bridge in Europe.* London: Headline, 2001.

Platt, Colin. *The English Medieval Town.* New York: David McKay, 1976.

Plucknett, T. F. T. *Statutes and Their Interpretation in the First Half of the Fourteenth Century.* Cambridge: Cambridge University Press, 1922.

Plunkett, Horace Curzon. *Rural Life Problems in the United States: Notes of an Irish Observer.* [1904.] New York: Macmillan, 1906.

Ponge, Francis. *The Making of the Pré.* Trans. Lee Fahnestock. Columbia: University of Missouri Press, 1979.

Poortinga, Ype. *De ring fan it ljocht.* Baarn, Netherlands: Bosch en Keuning, 1976.

Poortinga, Ype. *It fleanend skip: Folkforhalen fan Steven de Bruin.* Baarn, Netherlands: Bosch en Keuning, 1977.

Portuondo, María. *Secret Science: Spanish Cosmography and the New World*. Chicago: University of Chicago Press, 2009.

Powicke, M. *Military Obligation in Medieval England*. Oxford: Oxford University Press, 1962.

Quinn, David B. "Columbus and the North: England, Ireland, and Iceland." *William and Mary Quarterly* 49 (April 1992): 278–297.

Rae, John Bell. *The Road and the Car in American Life*. Cambridge, MA: MIT Press, 1971.

Raisz, Erwin. *Atlas of Global Geography*. New York: Harper, 1944.

Ray, John. *A Collection of English Words Not Generally Used*. London: Burrell, 1674.

Rees, Abraham. *The Cyclopaedia: or, Universal Dictionary of Arts, Sciences, and Literature*. 41 vols. Philadelphia: Bradford, 1805–1825.

Richardson, Charles. *A New Dictionary of the English Language*. 2 vols. London: Pickering, 1837.

Richeson, A. W. *English Land Measuring to 1800: Instruments and Practice*. Cambridge, MA: MIT Press, 1966.

Rigby, S. H. *Chaucer in Context*. Manchester: Manchester University Press, 1996.

Rippon, Stephen. "Focus or Frontier? The Significances of Estuaries in the Landscape of Southern Britain." *Landscapes* 8, no. 1 (2007): 23–38.

Roget, Peter Mark. *Thesaurus of English Words and Phrases*. [1852.] Boston: DeWolfe Fiske, c. 1859.

Role, Maurice. *L'étrange histoire des zeppelins*. Paris: France-Empire, 1972.

Rolt, L. T. C. *The Landscape Trilogy*. [1971, 1977, 1992.] Stroud, Gloucestershire: Sutton, 2005.

Rothfuss, Patrick. *The Name of the Wind*. New York: DAW, 2007.

Rothwell, Harry, ed. *English Historical Documents*. 6 vols. London: Eyre and Spottiswoode, 1975.

Roupnel, Gaston. *Histoire de la campagne française*. Paris: Bernard Grasset, 1932.

Roux, Jean-Michel. *Territoire sans lieux: La banalisation planifiée des régions*. Paris: Dunod, 1980.

Ruddock, Alwyn A. "Columbus and Iceland: New Light on an Old Problem." *Geographical Journal* 136 (June 1970): 177–189.

Schäfer, Jürgen. *Early Modern English Lexicography: A Survey of Monolingual Printed Glossaries and Dictionaries, 1475–1640: Additions and Corrections to the OED*. 2 vols. Oxford: Oxford University Press, 1989.

Schneider, Helmut J., ed. *Deutsche Landschaft*. Frankfurt: Insel, 1981.

Shipley, Joseph T. *Dictionary of Word Origins*. New York: Philosophical Library, 1945.

Siewers, Alfred Kentigern, ed. *Re-Imagining Nature: Environmental Humanities and Ecosemiotics*. Lewisburg, PA: Bucknell University Press, 2014.

Silver, Harry R. "Ethnoart." *Annual Review of Anthropology* 8 (1979): 267–307.

Simo, Melanie L. *Literature of Place: Dwelling on the Land before Earth Day 1970*. Charlottesville: University of Virginia Press, 2005.

Simpson, Jacqueline. "God's Visible Judgments: The Christian Dimensions of Landscape Legends." *Landscape History* 8 (1986): 53–58.

Skeat, Walter W. *An Etymological Dictionary of the English Language*. [1881.] Oxford: Clarendon Press, 1935.

Smyth, William Henry. *Sailor's Word-Book*. [1867.] London: Conway Maritime, 1991.

Solnit, Rebecca. *A Field Guide to Getting Lost*. New York: Penguin, 2005.

Sorden, Leland George. *Lumberjack Lingo*. Spring Green, WI: Wisconsin House, 1969.

Spenser, Edmund. *The Faerie Queene*. In *Poetical Works*, ed. J. C. Smith and E. De Selincourt. Oxford: Oxford University Press, 1924.

Spirn, Anne Whiston. *The Language of Landscape*. New Haven: Yale University Press, 1998.

Statutes of the Realm: Printed by Command of His Majesty King George the Third. 9 vols. London: George Eyre and Andrew Strahan, 1810–1822.

Stechow, Wolfgang. *Dutch Landscape Painting of the Seventeenth Century*. New York: Hacker, 1980.

Sticker, Georg. *Abhandlungen aus der Seuchengeschichte*. 2 vols. Giessen, Germany: Töpelmann, 1908–1912.

Stilgoe, John R. *Alongshore*. New Haven: Yale University Press, 1994.

Stilgoe, John R. *Borderland: Origins of the American Suburb, 1820–1939*. New Haven: Yale University Press, 1988.

Stilgoe, John R. *Common Landscape of America, 1580 to 1845*. New Haven: Yale University Press, 1982.

Stilgoe, John R. *Landscape and Images*. Charlottesville: University of Virginia Press, 2005.

Stilgoe, John R. *Lifeboat: A History of Courage, Cravenness, and Survival at Sea*. Charlottesville: University of Virginia Press, 2003.

Stilgoe, John R. *Metropolitan Corridor: Railroads and the American Scene*. New Haven: Yale University Press, 1983.

Stilgoe, John R. *Old Fields: Photography, Glamour, and Fantasy Landscape*. Charlottesville: University of Virginia Press, 2014.

Stilgoe, John R. *Outside Lies Magic: Regaining History and Awareness in Everyday Places*. New York: Walker, 1998.

Stilgoe, John R. *Shallow-Water Dictionary: A Grounding in Estuary English.* [1990.] New York: Princeton Architectural Press, 2008.

Taylor, Christopher. "*The Making of the English Landscape* and Beyond: Inspiration Dissemination." *Landscapes* 6, no. 2 (2005): 96–104.

Tennyson, Julian. *Suffolk Scene: A Book of Description and Adventure.* London: Blackie and Son, 1939.

Thoen, Erik, and Leen van Molle. *Rural History in the North Sea Area: An Overview of Recent Research, Middle Ages to Twentieth Century.* Turnhout, Belgium: Brepols, 2006.

Thomas, Richard. *An Historical Essay on the Magna Charta.* London: Mayor, 1829.

Thornton, Dora. *The Scholar in His Study: Ownership and Experience in Renaissance Italy.* New Haven: Yale University Press, 1997.

Thygesen, Lone, and George Blecher, eds. *Swedish Folktales and Legends.* New York: Pantheon, 1993.

Tolkien, J. R. R. *The Lord of the Rings.* [1954–1955.] 3 vols. New York: Ballantine, 1965.

Tomeï, Karel. *De bovenkant van Nederland: Holland from the Top.* Schiedam, Netherlands: Scriptum, 2012.

Tuan, Yi-Fu. *Landscapes of Fear.* New York: Pantheon, 1979.

Tuan, Yi-Fu. *Space and Place: The Perspective of Experience.* Minneapolis: University of Minnesota Press, 1977.

Tuan, Yi-Fu. *Topophilia: A Study of Environmental Perception, Attitudes, and Values.* Englewood Cliffs, NJ: Prentice-Hall, 1974.

Turner, R. V. *Judges, Administrators, and the Common Law in Angevin England.* London: Hambledon, 1994.

Turner, William. *The First and Seconde Partes of the Herbal.* [1551.] Collen [Cologne]: Birckman, 1568.

United States Navy. *American Practical Navigator*. Washington, DC: Government Printing Office, 1962.

Van der Stadt, Leontine. *Nederland in zeven overstromingen*. Zutphen: Walberg, 2013.

Van Vleck, Jennifer. *Empire of the Air: Aviation and the American Ascendancy*. Cambridge, MA: Harvard University Press, 2013.

Violet, Charles. *Solitary Journey*. London: Rupert Hart-Davis, 1954.

Warnke, Martin. *Political Landscape: The Art History of Nature*. Cambridge, MA: Harvard University Press, 1995.

Waters, Brian. *Severn Tide*. London: Dent, 1947.

Waters, D. W. *The Rutters of the Sea: The Sailing Directions of Pierre Garcie*. New Haven: Yale University Press, 1967.

Weber, Ferdinand A. *Handwörterbuch der deutschen Sprache*. [1842.] Rev. ed. Leipzig: Tauchniss, 1892.

Webster, Noah. *An American Dictionary of the English Language*. New York: S. Converse, 1828.

Webster, Noah. *A Compendious Dictionary of the English Language*. New Haven: Hudson and Goodwin, 1806.

Webster's New International Dictionary of the English Language. Springfield, MA: Merriam-Webster, 1934.

Weigand, L. K. *Deutsches Wörterbuch*. 2 vols. Giessen, Germany: Alfred Töpelmann, 1910.

Wells, H. G. *War in the Air: And Particularly How Mr. Bert Smallways Fared While It Lasted*. London: G. Bell and Sons, 1908.

Went, F. W. "Blue Hazes in the Atmosphere." *Nature* 187 (August 1960): 641–642.

Werrett, Simon. *Fireworks: Pyrotechnic Arts and Sciences in European History*. Chicago: University of Chicago Press, 2010.

Whiteley, George. *Northern Seas, Hardy Sailors*. New York: Norton, 1982.

Wiemann, Elsbeth, Jenny Gaschke, and Mona Stocker. *Die Entdeckung der Landschaft: Meisterwerke der niederländischen Kunst des 16. und 17. Jahrhunderts*. Stuttgart: Staatsgalerie, 2006.

William, Eurwyn. "The Protection of the House: Some Iconographic Evidence from Wales." *Folklore* 89, pt. 2 (1978): 148–153.

Williams, Ann, ed. *Domesday Book: A Complete Translation*. London: Penguin, 2003.

Williams, Glyndwr. *The Great South Sea: English Voyages and Encounters, 1570–1750*. New Haven: Yale University Press, 1997.

Willinsky, John. *Empire of Words: The Reign of the OED*. Princeton: Princeton University Press, 1994.

Wise, Hugh D. "Experiments with Kites." *Century Magazine* 54 (May 1897): 78–85.

Wood, Denis, and John Fels. *The Natures of Maps: Cartographic Constructions of the Natural World*. Chicago: University of Chicago Press, 2008.

Wood, Marion, ed. *The Hearth in Scotland*. Rosemarkie, U.K.: Scottish Vernacular Building Works Group, 2001.

Wright, Laura. *Sources of London English: Medieval Thames Vocabulary*. Oxford: Clarendon Press, 1996.

Wynne, Edward. *Growing Up Suburban*. Austin: University of Texas Press, 1977.

Zinsser, Hans. *Rats, Lice, and History*. Boston: Atlantic Monthly, 1935.